I0024250

Thomas Kennedy

A History of the Irish Protest Against Over-Taxation

1853-1897

Thomas Kennedy

A History of the Irish Protest Against Over-Taxation
1853-1897

ISBN/EAN: 9783744730792

Printed in Europe, USA, Canada, Australia, Japan

Cover: Foto ©ninafisch / pixelio.de

More available books at **www.hansebooks.com**

A HISTORY

OF THE

IRISH PROTEST AGAINST OVER-TAXATION,

FROM 1853 TO 1897.

BY

THOMAS KENNEDY,

B.A., ROYAL UNIVERSITY OF IRELAND;

BARRISTER-AT-LAW;

FITZGIBBON GOLD MEDALLIST AND O'HAGAN GOLD MEDALLIST OF THE LAW STUDENTS
DEBATING SOCIETY OF IRELAND;

*For some time Honorary Secretary to the All-Ireland Committee of the
Financial Relations League.*

DUBLIN :

HODGES, FIGGIS, & CO., Ltd., GRAFTON STREET,

BOOKSELLERS TO THE UNIVERSITY.

LONDON : SIMPKIN, MARSHALL, HAMILTON, KENT, & CO.

1897.

CONTENTS.

APPENDIX.

PREFACE.

THE Royal Commission on the Financial Relations of Great Britain and Ireland, appointed by Her Majesty's warrant on the 26th May, 1894, reported in the autumn of 1896 that the increase of taxation laid on Ireland between 1853 and 1860 was not justified by the then existing circumstances. The increase amounted to between two and three millions sterling per annum, and has been since levied. It was secured by the imposition of income tax and succession duties in 1853, and by the increase of stamp and spirit duties between 1853 and 1860. This augmented taxation was in excess of Ireland's just relative contribution to the Imperial Exchequer, and a violation of her constitutional rights under the Treaty of Union. No more inopportune time could have been chosen for imposing it. A famine, the most dire which has stricken a European country in the nineteenth century, had but recently devastated the land. Commerce and manufactures had commenced that decline which has continued to this day. The injurious effects of the Free Trade policy and repeal of the Corn Laws were already apparent, and population had commenced to fly from the country.

No weightier task devolves on a statesman than that of safeguarding the finances of his country. What must its plight be when a nation has no control over its taxation? The Treasury representatives, whom the Act for the Amalgamation of the Exchequers seemed to secure to Ireland, have long disappeared. The fiscal

policy of the empire has been shaped quite independently of the generally ineffectual votes of the Irish
representatives. Though powerless to prevent it, did
they not protest against the imposition of the unjustifiable burden of 1853-60? Did they not unceasingly
attempt to have it removed ?

Mr. Arthur J. Balfour said at Manchester, on the 9th
January, 1897, that it was only in October or November,
1896, that the Irish discovered that England was rob-
bing them of about £2,700,000 a year for fifty years.
Some notable Irishmen spent their lives trying to con-
vince England of this. Not an echo of the taxation
miserere which the Irish chanted for the past forty
years reached Mr. Balfour. General Dunne, Lord
Claud Hamilton, Robert Longfield, Q.C., Joseph Fisher,
John Blake Dillon, the O'Conor Don, Sir Joseph N.
M'Kenna, O'Neill Daunt, Mitchell Henry, and Isaac
Butt have written their names in the history of Ireland
by the attitude they took up on its taxation. The First
Lord of the Treasury, who was a Chief Secretary for
Ireland, never heard of them. A knowledge of Irish
history seems not to be essential to a ruler of Ireland.
Though English members fled the House of Commons
whenever the question of Irish taxation was raised, the
subject nevertheless pursued them in *The Times*. It
is sad to see justice delayed and defeated ; sadder after
repeated refusals to hear it denied that it was ever
claimed. Irishmen, in and out of the House of Commons, have protested against over-taxation during the
past forty years. If Sisyphus, in addition to doing his
own work, were loaded with the burden of Atlas, his
task would then be comparable to theirs. They had to
penetrate the Cimmerian darkness which enveloped the
Treasury accounts, and then essay the hopeless task of
convincing the inconvincibility of England. The increase
of taxation was accompanied by a concealment of its

incidence and amount. The Irish golden fleece was both stolen and hidden. The Treasury exacted all it could, then suppressed the amount, and mystified the account. When the Irish members became excessively clamorous, some occasional scraps of information were doled out to them. Whenever they put their case for redress before Parliament, they were met either with denial, evasion, or spurious political economy. The Treasury, like the wolf in Aesop's fable, changed its attitude as often as it was disconcerted by the force of truth. The loss of an argument only stimulated it to find a new one. According to Mr. W. E. Gladstone, taxation had nothing to do with the poverty of Ireland. Sir Stafford Northcote admitted that Ireland was the most heavily taxed country in Europe. He did not see his way to remedy it, as the burdens of the poorer districts of Great Britain would be thereby increased. Mr. Lowe's doctrine of individual taxation was afterwards preached from the front benches of the House of Commons and the leading columns of *The Times*. It held the field for years, and died hard. In the sixties and the seventies English financial authorities, from Mr. Gladstone down, denied that expenditure had anything to do with taxation. Now their trump card is that expenditure is a set-off against over-taxation. They refuse to apply this new-found test to the past, as the balance would then go against them. They are consistent in nothing but in exacting the last penny out of Ireland.

For twenty years—from 1853 to 1873—the Irish Conservative members led the way in whatever protests were made. When the wrong grew hoary, its custody passed from them and became the heritage of the Nationalists, who made all they could of it whenever a lull in their other occupations gave them leisure. Trinity College, Dublin, is often supposed by

Great Britain could be raised by an income tax of 2s. 6d. in the pound ; whilst an income tax of 5s. 3d. would be necessary to raise in Ireland its imperial taxation. In 1887 he proved that the imperial taxes of England other than the income tax were *five* times the income tax, of Scotland *seven* times, and of Ireland *twelve* times.

The Irish case against over-taxation was proved again and again in the House of Commons during the past thirty years. The Royal Commission has merely affirmed it on appeal, and vindicated the motives and action of the men who made it. England cannot plead prescription. The Irish claim for justice was made too frequently and too comprehensively to be barred by any statute of limitation. The Royal Commission has not yet brought redress. "Who would be free themselves must strike the blow."

Appeals for a union of Irishmen on this question were often made. They came first from the Conservative ranks. General Dunne, one of the upper class Irish Protestant gentry ; Joseph Fisher, a typical middle class Irish Protestant Dissenter; and Robert Longfield, a distinguished Protestant Conservative Irish lawyer, asked for a union of Irishmen to settle the proper taxa-tion of the country. Similar appeals came from the Nationalist ranks. O'Neill Daunt, the veteran Repealer; John Blake Dillon, the amnestied Young Irelander; and Isaac Butt, the moderate and constitutional Home Rule leader, declared that it was the duty of all Irishmen to co-operate in reducing taxation. At the present day there has been a wonderful union of all classes of the Irish people at public meetings and at public boards; but though men differing as much as Mr. Healy, Mr. Lecky, Mr. Horace Plunkett, Mr. Redmond, and Col. Saunderson strove to promote united action in the House of Commons, they were not successful.

I have endeavoured to show, I hope not without some success, that excessive taxation was imposed and perpetuated on Ireland in defiance of the oft-repeated protests of her representatives; that public opinion in Ireland at an early stage adequately recognised what a grievous oppression this taxation was ; and that the harsh and unyielding attitude of successive ministries during the past forty years leaves no room for doubt that no more serious and difficult problem confronts the Irish people than that of securing the restitution and readjustment of this excessive taxation.

I have in many instances quoted the *ipsissima verba* of speeches, resolutions, motions, &c. I trust that this book will be found more useful on that account.

I have to express my thanks to the Right Honourable the O'Conor Don, Sir J. N. M'Kenna, Mr. Mitchell Henry, and Mr. Charles Dawson for lending me publications which have materially assisted me. I am also much indebted to Mr. James MacIvor, of the King's Inns Library, and Mr. T. W. Lyster, of the National Library of Ireland.

THOMAS KENNEDY.

9 Brookfield Terrace,
    Donnybrook, Dublin,
        18th November, 1897.

WORKS ON IRISH TAXATION.

HOW IRELAND MAY BE SAVED. By Joseph Fisher. London: Ridgway, 1862.

THE CASE OF IRELAND; TOGETHER WITH SOME LETTERS ON THE EXCESSIVE TAXATION OF IRELAND. By Joseph Fisher. London: Ridgway, 1863.

REPORT OF THE SPECIAL COMMITTEE OF THE MUNICIPAL COUNCIL OF DUBLIN ON THE STATE OF THE PUBLIC ACCOUNTS BETWEEN IRELAND AND GREAT BRITAIN. Dublin: Dollard, 1863.

DEBT AND TAXATION OF IRELAND. By Joseph J. Murphy. Reports of the Statistical and Social Inquiry Society of Ireland. Dublin: Ponsonby, 1864.

THE IRISH TAXATION COMMITTEE. By The O'Conor Don, m.p. Dublin: Fowler, 1865.

FINANCIAL RELATIONS BETWEEN GREAT BRITAIN AND IRELAND, AND THE PRESSURE OF TAXATION UPON IRISH RESOURCES. By W. J. O'N. Daunt. Dublin: Robert Chapman, 1873.

THE FINANCIAL AND ECONOMICAL CONDITION OF IRELAND. By Mitchell Henry, m.p. Dublin: Irish Home Rule League, 1875.

THE INCIDENCE OF IMPERIAL TAXATION ON IRELAND. By Sir Joseph Neale M'Kenna, m.p. Dublin: Irish Home Rule League, 1876.

IMPERIAL TAXATION: THE CASE OF IRELAND PLAINLY STATED. By Sir Joseph M'Kenna, m.p. London: Rivingtons, 1883.

FISCAL RELATIONS OF THE UNITED KINGDOM AND IRELAND. By William F. Bailey. Dublin: Hodges, Figgis, & Co., 1886.

THE IRISH LAND QUESTION; OR, IRELAND, THE PROCESS OF EXHAUSTION, 1801 TO 1880 (BOTH INCLUSIVE), EXAMINED AND EXPLAINED. By Sir Joseph M'Kenna, m.p. London: Ridgway, 1887.

THE FINANCIAL RELATIONS OF GREAT BRITAIN AND
IRELAND. By AN IRISHMAN. Dublin: *Freeman's Journal*, 1892.

ENGLAND'S WEALTH IRELAND'S POVERTY. By THOMAS
LOUGH, M.P. London: Downey, 1896.

ENGLAND'S DEBT TO IRELAND. By J. P. MAUNSELL, M.A.
Dublin: *Daily Express*, 1897.

THE OVER-TAXATION OF IRELAND: A RECORD OF
MEETINGS, 1896-97. Dublin: *Freeman's Journal*, 1897.

THE FINANCIAL RELATIONS QUESTION: EXPENDITURE
ACCOUNT. By A. W. SAMUELS, Q.C. Dublin: Sealy, Bryers,
& Walker, 1897.

SOME FEATURES OF THE OVER-TAXATION OF IRELAND.
By NICHOLAS J. SYNNOTT. Dublin: Sealy, Bryers, & Walker, 1897.

FINANCIAL RELATIONS BETWEEN GREAT BRITAIN AND
IRELAND. By THOMAS P. WHITTAKER, M.P. Hull: *Eastern
Morning News Co.*, 1897.

THE FINANCIAL RELATIONS OF GREAT BRITAIN AND
IRELAND. By SIR EDWARD CLARKE, Q.C. London: Stevens
and Haynes, 1897.

THE OVER-TAXATION OF IRELAND. By HON. EDWARD
BLAKE. M.P. Dublin: Sealy, Bryers, & Walker, 1897.

WORKS BY MR. W. J. O'NEILL DAUNT, IN WHICH
IRISH TAXATION IS MENTIONED.

EIGHTY-FIVE YEARS OF IRISH HISTORY. London: Ward
& Downey, 1886.

A LIFE SPENT FOR IRELAND. London: Fisher Unwin, 1897.

HISTORY

OF THE

IRISH PROTEST AGAINST OVER-TAXATION.

CHAPTER I.

A.D. 1853.

MAJOR-GENERAL FRANCIS PLUNKETT DUNNE.

ON the 18th April, 1853, Mr. W. E. Gladstone, who was Chancellor of the Exchequer in the Coalition Government of which Lord Aberdeen was Prime Minister, John Sadleir a Lord of the Treasury, and William Keogh Solicitor-General for Ireland, announced, when introducing the Budget, that he would extend the income tax to Ireland. The poverty of the country, the full measure in which it already contributed to imperial revenue, and the necessity, on grounds of public policy, of offering some inducements to absentee landlords to reside at home, had hitherto prevented its extension.

Knowledge after the event, which is everyone's, has made it clear that Ireland was face to face with a crisis fraught with disastrous consequences to her material well-being. It may be asked, how did her people demean themselves? and who amongst them made timely and opportune protest? Into the breach created by Mr. Gladstone stepped Major-General Francis Plunkett Dunne. The gage of battle cast down by the wizard of finance he instantly took up. Resistance to

B

and protest against the financial injustice done to his
country he made the great purpose of his life. Upheld
by his well-founded belief in the justice of his cause,
gallant soldier that he was, he led for years a forlorn
hope against the injustice and inconvincibility of
England. Unsuccessful in his objects and unappre-
ciated in his actions, time has more than amply
vindicated both. If ever there be a Pantheon of
distinguished Irishmen, his shall be no obscure corner
therein. His name shall ever be indissolubly associated
with the Irish protest against the over-taxation imposed
by Mr. Gladstone. On his father's side he traced his
descent in unbroken line from the ancient Irish chief-
tains of Brittas ; whilst his mother was sister to the first
Earl of Bantry. Born in 1802, he graduated in Trinity
College, Dublin, and entered the army as cornet in the
Dragoon Guards Retiring from the army in 1840,
he entered Parliament, and represented Portarlington
from 1847 to 1857, and the Queen's County from 1859
to 1868. A Conservative, he held office as Private
Secretary to Lord Eglinton when Lord Lieutenant of
Ireland in 1858-59. He died on 6th July, 1874, and
an obituary newspaper notice states that no man in
the Queen's County was more generally or deservedly
popular. In private life he was all that was estimable
—courteous, honourable, and upright, a perfect gentleman, beloved by the poor as well as by the rich, and
a thorough Irishman and lover of his country. All
those who held intercourse with him during his long
and honourable career were well aware of his sterling
honesty and worth.

   The Budget proposals of Mr. Gladstone which called
forth the opposition of General Dunne may be thus
briefly stated :—The revenue for 1852-53 showed a surplus of £2,460,000. A committee of the House of Lords
had recommended that the charges on the famine-

stricken districts of Ireland, amounting to £260,000 a
year, and called "Consolidated Annuities," should be
partially extinguished. It was a clear case for remission, and the surplus made it quite easy. Mr. Gladstone
remitted the "Annuities," but imposed the income tax.
For the shilling he gave away with his left hand he
exacted a pound with his right. General Dunne
attacked the new departure in fiscal policy on the
23rd May, 1853, by the following motion :—

> That it is expedient, before additional taxation be extended to
> Ireland, that a select committee be appointed to inquire into and
> consider the fiscal and political relations and relative taxation of
> Great Britain and Ireland, and to report whether the latter
> kingdom does not bear her fair share of imperial taxation.

The speech in which he introduced his motion was
one of great moderation ; and the justice and obvious
necessity of his proposal should have commended it to
Parliament. He foretold that this Budget would inflict
greater injury upon Ireland than any former Budget
that he remembered. He did not stand there to deny
that Ireland ought to bear her fair share of taxation—
he did not even at the moment say that the income tax
ought not to be extended to that country—but what he
contended was, that before Ireland was to be saddled
with a heavier load of taxation than she had hitherto
borne, a preliminary inquiry should take place into the
resources of the country ; and he further maintained
that, if they extended this tax to Ireland without first
instituting such an inquiry, they would be guilty of a
direct breach of the articles of the Act of Union. It
was now proposed to impose a burden of an additional half a million and upwards of taxation upon
Ireland by the introduction of the income tax, and
Ireland would not receive any benefit from the extra
charge. It was most unjust to call upon Ireland to

submit to this additional contribution without first
instituting this preliminary inquiry into her resources
relatively to England under the terms of the Act of
Union. The motion was seconded by Mr. Macartney,
who thought it the height of injustice in any Government to come forward with such a proposition as this,
which must be regarded as an aggravation of the
financial oppressions under which Ireland suffered.

Lord Claud Hamilton also supported General Dunne,
and the following notable protest was made by Mr.
John Francis Maguire, the Member for Dungarvan :—

The attempt to gull the people of Ireland into an approval of
this tax by saying that the present proposition was a good bargain,
because they would have to pay £460,000 instead of £260,000, to
which they were at present liable, was worse than a financial
juggle. It was, if he might say so in parliamentary language, an
Exchequer swindle. The trick was so stale, the juggle so plain,
and the real object so unconcealed, he could only express his
wonder at any man representing an Irish constituency being gulled
by it.

Mr. Maguire was in Parliament from 1852 to 1872,
and during those twenty years he was the popular
leader. His great sincerity, ability, and earnestness
were unselfishly devoted to the service of his country.
With the exception of the notable protest recorded
above, some minor references, and his evidence before
General Dunne's Committee, he does not seem to have
grasped the terrible reality of over-taxation, and to
what extent the material depression of the country
was due to it, but devoted himself to the solution of the
religious and agrarian problems of the Irish difficulty.

General Dunne's motion was met in the most hostile
manner by Mr. Gladstone, and though the Irish Conservative and Popular members united in urging on the
Government the expediency of this preliminary inquiry,
they were defeated, the voting being 61 for the motion
and 194 against.

WHEN Mr. Gladstone increased the taxation of Ireland in 1853, he was well aware of the state of the country, admitted the circumstances of the awful calamity which had lately visited it, and acknowledged that traces of it remained in many social and economic forms and in a burdensome debt. But all Ireland was not alike, and there were "*certain districts*" which did not need to shrink from their full taxation, and which had no reasonable claim or plea to offer for exemption. These words were no sooner uttered than forgotten. The extension of the income tax and the increase of the spirit duties were not confined to "*certain districts*," but applied to the whole island. The phrase "*certain districts*" covers all that has ever been since contended for in the phrases "*separate entity*" and "*geographical taxation.*" He argued that the new taxation would advance a great step towards establishing an equalization of taxation between the three countries. Having declared that he would remit the "consolidated annuities," impose the income tax, and increase the spirit duties, he plumed himself that he would thereby make a great stride towards advantages which he hardly knew how to appreciate—namely, bringing the two countries towards the establishment of the principle of "*equalized taxation.*" He brushed lightly aside all arguments founded on the poverty of the country, and utterly ignored her treaty rights.

The pretext he availed of to justify on principle the increase of Irish taxation was elevated by him into

an economic doctrine, and dignified with the name of
"*equalized taxation.*" It was reserved for a later period
to show how utterly unjust was his policy; how disastrous to the material condition of Ireland; how
his intentions failed, if they were such, to secure contributions proportioned to ability from Great Britain
and Ireland; and that his plausible and high-sounding
doctrine of "equalized taxation" was one of the most
fatal of economic heresies, and one made the pretext for
the most oppressive financial injustice to Ireland. The
taxes on commodities chiefly consumed by English-
men were levelled down year by year. Those on articles
principally used in Ireland were made heavier. This
duplex action was maintained for years for the impoverishment of Ireland and the enrichment of England.
No greater sophistry was ever preached than that of
"equalized taxation." It was the greatest engine of
oppression in Ireland during the second half of the
nineteenth century.

Neither can he be absolved of culpability for the evil
effects which followed. The consequences to Ireland
have been—without exaggeration—almost incalculable.
The taxation since raised was in excess of the country's
requirements and capacity. The amount contributed
for imperial services over and above local expenditure
in Ireland was, in 1859-60, £5,396,000; in 1869-70,
£4,488,210; in 1879-80, £3,226,307; and in 1889-90,
£2,676,970. An average of these sums is £3,946,872, or
in round numbers £4,000,000. The Irish contribution to
the Imperial Exchequer, over and above local expenditure, for the forty years from 1853 to 1893 amounted
to £160,000,000. All this money was spent out of the
country. It is only a little short of the war tribute
which France paid Germany. The policy of raising
more taxes than are required for necessary and essential
expenditure has at all times been condemned by sound

political economists. Mr. Gladstone when Chancellor of the Exchequer made the following statement on over-taxation in the House of Commons on 12th June, 1863 :—

I am very much inclined to question a proposition which I understood him to lay down—that taxation is no diminution of the wealth of a country, provided the money raised by its means is spent in the country in which it happens to be levied. I do not know that this is the time or place to discuss a point of political economy ; but I may observe that I regard that proposition as a fallacy. In my opinion, taxation which is unnecessary for the real purposes of government is an entire waste of public money, and leads to bad consequences, whether it is spent in the country in which it is levied or not.

If the consequences of an excessive revenue, even when spent within the country in which it is raised, are bad, how much more intensified the evils must be when the expenditure is made out of the country.

General Dunne's request for an inquiry was reason-able and just. Mr. Gladstone advanced no valid argument why it should not be entertained. There was no necessity for haste. No deficit had to be met. A desire to do what was just, rather than what was brilliant, would have prompted an examination of the condition of the country. Recent events bore heavily on Ireland. The establishment of the poor law system had added considerably to local burdens. The repeal of the Corn Laws rapidly destroyed the Irish export grain trade. The failure of the potato had caused the famine. Irish manufactures, with few exceptions, were declining. Land was going rapidly out of cultivation. The people were fleeing from the country. These were danger signals sufficient to cause the boldest of Chan-cellors of the Exchequer to pause. Yet heedless of all protests Mr. Gladstone persevered with his scheme.

The only bright spot in this dark chapter was that he intended that his new imposts should be temporary.

" The taxation we propose for Ireland would in the first two years be considerably higher than the taxation we propose to remove; but if we look to the time when, as I have said, Parliament will be in a position to part with the income tax, Ireland will enjoy, and enjoy for a long term of years, a much larger remission of consolidated annuities than it will have to bear of additional burdens in the shape of spirit duty."

Forty-four years have elapsed, during twenty-five of which Mr. Gladstone was a member of the Cabinet, and his promise remains unfulfilled.

CHAPTER III.

EVENTS IN A.D. 1860.

THE JIBES AND SNEERS OF "THE TIMES." GENERAL DUNNE APPEALS TO ALL IRISHMEN TO UNITE ON THE QUESTION.

The Irish Quarterly Review for January, 1860, contains an article on "The Debt and Taxation of Ireland." It appeared from a Parliamentary return, No. 159, issued in 1859, that the Irish contribution to the Imperial Exchequer for the last financial year was £8,800,000. Irish local expenditure for the same year amounted to £4,178,000. The surplus of revenue over expenditure remitted from Ireland to England was £4,462,000. The writer does not examine these figures in the light of over-taxation or economic drain, but deems them a complete answer to the sneers of *The Times* at Irish insolvency. The campaign of calumny against Ireland was so effectual that the writer merely plucked up courage enough to say that Ireland was paying her way, and was meeting every charge, just and unjust, necessary for her government. No bolder answer was yet attempted ; whilst the fact, which later investigation has made evident, that she was contributing far beyond her ability and her treaty rights to the Imperial Treasury was known to few in Ireland, so successful was the work of financial juggle and Treasury suppression.

The collection of extracts from *The Times* and other English papers printed in the article had considerable influence in directing Irish opinion to the question, and influencing by repulsion the movement soon commenced in Ireland and in Parliament. They are as follows :—

Rackrent landlords and exacting persons collect their dues by a soldiery paid by English taxes.—*Quarterly Review*.

The Treaty of Union with Ireland has already been, in more than one respect, materially modified. According to it, Ireland, besides providing for her own establishments, was to bear two-seventeenths of the entire public expenditure of the empire. But no part whatever of this condition has been fulfilled. Down to this hour Ireland has not (mainly because of her being afflicted with an overgrown alien Church) contributed one single shilling to the general expense.—*Courier*.

Look at the amount of taxes paid by Ireland generally, and see how she fulfils the terms of the Union contract. By that treaty she ought to contribute towards the revenue of the empire 3 (*sic*) parts out of 17. Taking the whole revenue of the United Kingdom at £48,000,800 in round numbers, 3-17ths (*sic*) would be something near £5,000,000, whereas the revenue raised in Ireland has not for some years past, as we hear, exceeded £5,000,000 or thereabouts. Yet Ireland has retained the whole of her representatives, though she has fallen short of her revenue by a third.—*Times*.

Ireland is a loss to this country. Her revenue does not cover her proportion of the debt and the expenses of her civil and military establishment.—*Times*.

Ireland is a trouble, a vexation, and an expense to this country. We must pay to feed it and keep it in order. We are paying its paupers, its labourers, its policemen, its sailors.—*Times*.

The Celt counts with the lame, the blind, the sick, the aged, and the insane as an impotent class.—*Times*.

We have hospitals, poor-houses, prisons, asylums, and Connaught.—*Times*.

For a whole generation the prolific wretchedness of the unreclaimed Celt has made Ireland a continual drain on the resources of this country, and for three years the burden of public benevolence has pressed with fearful force upon every industrious class of this island.—*Times*.

There is no sadder chapter in the literary history of the financial controversy between Great Britain and Ireland than the sustained and implacable hostility of *The Times* to the just claims of Ireland.

In the House of Commons, on 30th March, 1860, General Dunne renewed his protest, and appealed for a union of all classes in Ireland to settle the fair taxation of the country. He said he took the opportunity of protesting against the unfair taxation to which Ireland was subjected as compared with England, and which was quite opposed to the spirit and terms of the Act of Union. He estimated the imperial taxation at £9,000,000, and the absentee rent at £4,000,000. The Chancellor of the Exchequer had spoken of the increase of wealth as justifying the income tax. He denied that the wealth of Ireland was increasing : the returns showed it was diminishing ; 500,000 acres of land had gone out of cultivation since 1847 ; foreign imports and exports were less than in 1790. Where was the prosperity in Ireland to entitle the Chancellor of the Exchequer to add to its taxation? Money spent on the defence of England was no advantage to Ireland. He hoped that ere long every Irish Member would come to Parliament pledged to settle the fair proportion of taxation to be borne by Ireland; but until that arrangement was made every Irishman ought to object to any additional taxation whatever. He submitted that it was high time that taxation, as between Ireland and

England, should be settled on a proper basis, because at present he was perfectly satisfied that they paid what was not fair.

He received no support, and his motion to reduce the income tax for Ireland from tenpence to ninepence was defeated. The Chancellor of the Exchequer alone replied to him, and relied on his old argument of equal taxation.

Again, as in 1853, General Dunne was before his time. Though on all sides the evidence of Irish decline was accumulating, its true cause, owing to the fierce passions called into play by several political and religious questions, was not yet generally recognised.

CHAPTER IV.

A.D. 1862.

SERJEANT HERON, Q.C., ON IRISH DECAY.

"An unjust system of taxation does not, any more than poisoning of the blood by impure air, forthwith evince its specific action ; the operation is nevertheless deadly, because it is continuous and the evil cumulative."

For nine years Ireland had borne the increased burdens imposed in 1853. The spirit duties had swept most of the distilleries from the land, and the income tax was the last straw which forced many a nobleman and gentleman into the Incumbered Estates Court. The steady drain of capital had indirectly crippled almost every industry. National decay and decline were apparent to all, but are nowhere better shown than in the writings of a distinguished Irish lawyer.

Denis Caulfield Heron, Q.C., LL.D., was a brilliant student of Trinity College, Dublin, Professor of Jurisprudence in the Queen's College, Galway, and Bencher of the King's Inn. He was third Serjeant-at-Law, and an accomplished writer on constitutional history and jurisprudence. In a paper read before the *Statistical and Social Inquiry Society of Ireland* on 20th January, 1862, he made the following remarks on the then condition of Ireland :—

" The decrease of the Irish population, as regards the original number, as regards the number of square miles in the country, and as regards the historical features of the case, there being neither civil war nor religious persecution, is perfectly unparalleled in ancient or modern history.

" The rental of Ireland is less in 1861 than it was in 1805. The wealth of the country is decreasing. A progressive decrease in population and in the production of wealth is a sign that something is not right in the legal and social conditions of a country. Population is everywhere proportioned to the means of subsistence. And the decrease in the cultivation of the land, and the decrease in the number of domestic animals in Ireland, have now rapidly commenced upon the decrease of population being accomplished. Men decay, but wealth does not accumulate.

" The population that has remained in Ireland has deteriorated from the year 1841. The best educated, the most energetic of the peasants have emigrated during the last fifteen years. Population is not the sole test of prosperity—it is one of the tests. Production of wealth is not the sole test of prosperity—it is one of the tests.

" The diminution of population, the diminution of cultivation, the diminution of domestic animals in Ireland, all show that in the present struggle for existence, which nations as well as individuals undergo, Ireland is beaten.

" One of the causes of the decrease of production is

that the best of the peasantry under the present system emigrate.

"For various reasons the Poor Law system has not worked well in Ireland. It has been one of the prominent causes in late years of the degradation of the peasantry.

"But whilst the peasantry have declined in numbers, have the upper classes in consequence been prosperous? From October, 1849, to August, 1859, the gross amount produced by sales in the Incumbered Estates Court was £25,190,839. The exultation manifested at the disappearance of the Irish peasantry is easily to be explained by what Savigny terms the foreign historical causes. But I have never been able to understand the exultation manifested at the enormous amount of ruin amongst the aristocracy and gentry of Ireland which these figures demonstrate. I regret that so many Irish gentlemen are annihilated off the soil of Ireland.

"It is asserted that the prosperity of Ireland is rapidly and progressively increasing for the last sixty years, certainly for the last fifteen years. One of the alleged scientific tests of progressive prosperity is the enormous number of ruined peers and gentry sold out by the Incumbered Estates Court.

"The number of the professional and educated classes in Ireland is diminishing. The number of students annually entering Trinity College from 1845 to 1849 averaged 351. During the last few years it has averaged 290.

"The number of practising barristers is rapidly diminishing. In 1788 the names of 622 barristers appeared in the Dublin Directory. The number of barristers paying their subscriptions to the Law Library of the Four Courts amounted to 690 in the year 1850. In 1861 it amounted to 427.

"County society is vanishing out of Ireland. There

are more ruins of castles and abbeys in Clare and
Galway than there are gentlemen's houses inhabited by
a resident proprietary.

"As compared with the progress of Europe, Ireland
is now a much less desirable place to live in than it
was at the commencement of the nineteenth century.
Under the present system it will continue every year
to be a less desirable place to live in."

CHAPTER V.

A.D. 1863.

GENERAL DUNNE REFUSED AN INQUIRY.

THE alarming decay so evident in Ireland, and the
growing belief that over-taxation was the chief cause,
found expression in the House of Commons on
12th June, 1863, when General Dunne moved—

That a select committee be appointed to inquire into the causes
of the present depressed condition of Ireland and the effects of
the taxation she now bears.

He stated that he had desired to bring the motion
on earlier in the session, but was prevented by the
death of Sir George C. Lewis. He scornfully alluded
to the small attendance of members as certain proof
that the House of Commons took little interest in the
condition of Ireland. Notwithstanding the statements
daily made of the fabulous growth of prosperity in
Ireland, he asserted that the improvement of the
country was not as great as might have been expected.
He emphatically deprecated the idea that he entertained
any wild views of violently interfering with the Union ;
but he held that the only basis on which it could be

maintained was that of mutual interest and perfect
equality. He enumerated amongst the indications of
the impoverishment of Ireland—first, the diminution
of the population, which could not be attributed to any
want of industry of the people, for they prospered
elsewhere ; second, the decay of agriculture exhibited
by the falling-off in the area under cultivation, representing an annual loss of £10,000,000. As almost
everything in Ireland depended on agriculture, its decay
meant universal depression. The decrease in live stock
between 1856 and 1860 represented a loss of £12,000,000.
Green crops and potatoes were going out of cultivation.
The foreign import and export trade was greater at the
time of the Union than it was then. There was a
continual decrease in the number of mills and of the
persons employed therein. The Chancellor of the
Exchequer, in his financial statement, had admitted
that capital in Ireland was diminishing and that distress
prevailed, to which General Dunne replied that there
was only one thing increasing in Ireland, and that was
taxation. It was estimated that the customs, excise,
stamps, inland revenue, and income tax yielded about
£7,000,000 ; but he believed the actual taxation was
higher. He quoted from Lord Castlereagh, Sir Robert
Peel, Mr. Corry, Mr. James Fitzgerald, Mr. Parnell,
Mr. Wellesley Poole, who had all protested that Ireland
was not called upon to submit to an excessive amount
of taxation beyond what she was able to bear. The
consolidation of the Exchequers in 1817 was not an
equalization of taxation. Seeing that the taxation of
Ireland had been at various periods one-twelfth, one-
seventh, and one-tenth of the imperial taxation, and
that up to the present moment there had been no
re-adjustment, he charged the English Government
with a glaring infraction of the Treaty of Union. The
Irish had a right to a re-adjustment of their taxation.

He hoped the House would take the matter into consideration, in order to determine whether Ireland was
justly or unjustly taxed. They were bound by the
Act of Union to treat Ireland fairly, and that had never
yet been done. Some of the returns issued were plainly
and palpably false. What he wished was to have some
means by which to arrive at a proximate rate of fair
taxation and apportionment of the debt due by each
country. Was it not fair that a re-adjustment of debt
and proportion of taxation should even now, at the third
recurrence of the stipulated period, be made? Ireland
suffered from the immense pressure of taxation, and
that was one principal reason why the country was
exhausted of its capital. A great portion of the
taxation of Ireland was drawn out of the country and
spent in England. Little of the imperial revenue was
spent out of England, and expenditure there on dock-
yards, arsenals, and public works benefited the working
classes. The drain of taxation from Ireland was continual, and there was also the annual drain of the
incomes of absentees. He was certain that, as long as
the present system of taxation was pursued with regard
to Ireland, her condition would not materially improve.
He regretted to see the population of Ireland falling off,
and that many of her industrious sons were flying to
other countries. He concluded by apologizing to the
House that a soldier was not, perhaps, the best fitted
to deal with the question.

The Irish members who supported General Dunne in
this debate were Mr. Robert Longfield, Q.C., Conservative member for Mallow ; Mr. W. H. Gregory, Conservative Member for County Galway ; Mr. W. H. F. Cogan,
Liberal Member for Kildare ; the Right Hon. James
Whiteside, Conservative Member for Trinity College,
and afterwards Chief Justice of Ireland ; and Mr. John
Francis Maguire, the popular or Independent Opposition

Member for Dungarvan. The demand for inquiry into the taxation of the country was made and most strongly supported by Conservative members.

Mr. Longfield said that a debt of gratitude was due by everyone connected with Ireland to General Dunne, who must have impressed the House with the fairness of his views, and the sincerity with which he put them forward. Test his figures in every possible way, they established that there had been a decrease in the funded property of Ireland, a decrease in her agricultural produce, a decrease in live stock, and ultimately a decrease in the population. From 1852 to the present time the growth of taxation had been rapid and uniform, and the country had drooped under the additional burden. Blame could not be laid upon the law of landlord and tenant, the grand juries, or the Established Church, for these had been in existence prior to 1852, and in spite of them the prosperity of Ireland was progressive. The change must be sought in events subsequent to 1852. Taxation alone had increased since then. With the single exception of the assessed taxes, the uttermost strain of fiscal imposition had been put upon the weakness of Ireland. Taxation had been actually doubled in ten years. A few years ago there were ninety-five distilleries in Ireland. Mr. Gladstone's system of taxation had already reduced them to twenty-five. The relative proportion of the taxation ought to be adjusted according to the articles of the Union. General Dunne had said that taxation had a great deal to do with the decline of prosperity in Ireland, and the remission of taxation might have a great deal to do with a revival of prosperity.

Mr. Whiteside supported General Dunne. He did not ask for inequality of taxation, but, considering the admitted distress in Ireland, was it not reasonable to inquire whether Ireland was able to bear, in her present

C

position, the amount of taxation imposed on her, and
then to inquire whether the taxation might not generally
be reduced as regards the whole empire. It would be
an important result of this motion if the representatives
of Ireland were obliged to look into the general taxation of the country, and seek for a common remedy by
the diminution of the common burden. He then ironi-
cally remarked that nothing was so fertilizing, nothing
so improving, as the increase of the burden of taxation.
It was no answer to the present request for an inquiry
to mention taxation not pressed upon Ireland. Taxation must be regulated according to the ability of the
country to bear it. It was unwise to oppress the energies
and exhaust the resources of a nation.

Mr. Gladstone, who was Chancellor of the Exchequer,
replied for the Government. He was glad that the
question had been brought seriously before the House.
He demurred to General Dunne's arguments. Whilst
there was distress in Ireland, it could not be ascribed to
taxation. There was no proof or presumption that
fiscal injustice was done to Ireland. He presumed that
General Dunne would not press for the appointment of
a select committee, which would excite hopes, but make
little progress with an inquiry involving so many details.
He did not deny there was distress in Ireland, but he
believed the interruption to her recent great and real
progress would soon disappear.

The statement of the intentions of the Government
was decisive, and the motion was negatived without a
division.

The Morning Post (London), in an article on the
debate, admitted that it was a melancholy fact that the
prosperity of Ireland, so far from increasing, had been
on the wane during the past three or four years. Whatever might be the remedy for the present condition of
affairs in Ireland, it did not lie, as seemed to have been

suggested by General Dunne, in a revised system of
taxation in Ireland, or the expenditure therein of a
large amount of the public revenues.

The Times, having taken forty-eight hours to consider,
praised the Irish Members for the tone, temper, and
moderation with which they had debated the motion.
Having made some remarks on the fertility of the
country, emigration, the Established Church, and lack
of prosperity, it proceeded :—

A more important issue was raised by Colonel Dunne when he
undertook to show that Ireland was taxed more heavily than
England and Scotland. It required some boldness to raise this
question, for it always has been accepted as a settled fact that
Ireland had, in the adjustment of this imperial taxation, been
placed in a position of advantage to which no part of an empire
has a right while it is permitted to enjoy absolute political equality.
. . . . But the facts now stand confessed that, even of the
taxes she does pay, Ireland pays very much less than England
per man ; that she has many exemptions to which she has no
right, for they are exemptions from taxation on luxuries and
property, which are alike capable of paying taxes in poor as in
rich countries ; and, further, that a larger proportion of public
money is spent in Ireland than is spent in England or Scotland,
having regard to the money raised in each country, and to the
respective populations. This demonstration is complete ; it has
been made in the face of the world, and has been found unanswerable. We hope that this part of the question is set at
rest for ever.

The Times in the *rôle* of a prophet on Ireland was
more ludicrous than ever Mother Shipton had been.
So far from the question being set at rest for ever, a
movement had already commenced in Ireland which
forced the taxation question so rapidly to the front that,
despite the great civil war in the United States, the
French war in Mexico, and the cotton famine in
Lancashire, it largely engrossed the attention of Parliament during the two succeeding years.

CHAPTER VI.

A.D. 1863.

JOHN BLAKE DILLON.

THE protest which the Irish Conservative Members were making against over-taxation was to become general in Ireland, and receive all the impetus which an aroused public opinion can give it, owing to the action of a great popular leader. After the amnesty of the Young Ireland chiefs, John Blake Dillon returned from exile in America to Dublin. For some time he confined himself to his practice at the Bar, but later on entered the Municipal Corporation of Dublin as Councillor for the Wood Quay Ward. Duffy, in *Young Ireland*, says of him, that all his studies and projects had direct relation to the people. Codes, tenures, and social theories were his familiar reading. He saw with burning impatience the wrongs inflicted on the industrious poor. He desired a national existence primarily to get rid of social degradation and suffering. *The Times* said of him that, though he held extreme views on Irish politics, he was respected by all parties as an honourable, upright, truthful, and earnest man, and that everyone who knew him felt that he acted from conviction and a sincere love of his country. The practical bent of his genius, and his intense yearnings for the economic prosperity of Ireland, naturally attracted him to the over-taxation question, which he determined to raise in the Municipal Council. Accordingly, he had a special meeting of that body summoned on the 21st April, 1863. To a full chamber, in an earnest, passionate speech, replete with arguments and facts, he laid bare the financial wrongs perpetrated on Ireland since the Union. He read the extracts from

The Times quoted in Chapter III, and inveighed against their coarseness and calumny. The financial problem of the moment could be solved by the answers to two questions. First, Was Ireland now charged with a just and fair proportion of the expenditure of the empire, and no more? Second, To what extent were Irish taxes expended in Ireland, and how far might they be regarded as a tribute raised in this country to be expended elsewhere? It seemed to him that one of the worst features of the case was that, whilst expenditure in Ireland remained stationary, her burdens increased with marvellous rapidity. The taxation of Ireland had been enormously increased, whilst the increase of home expenditure was comparatively insignificant. He alluded to the overwhelming evidences of Irish decay visible on all sides; and, in conclusion, urged that the time was favourable for redress, as the Chancellor of the Exchequer, having a large surplus, could afford to be just. He submitted that the abolition of the income tax in Ireland would not be more than a due compensation for the injustice it had sustained. In the debate which followed ten members of the Council joined. Party feeling ran high when allusion was made to other questions of the hour, but ultimately Mr. Dillon's motion for an inquiry into the public accounts of Great Britain and Ireland was carried unanimously. The notable protest which the Corporation were about to make was almost entirely Mr. Dillon's work. The lucid and convincing case which he presented united on this occasion members of a Council divided on many burning party social and religious questions. With foresight and wisdom, he selected the Council Hall of Dublin as the best vantage-point available from which to give the widest publication to his conclusions and belief on over-taxation. He clearly realized the economic evils of which it was the root, and desired the union of all Irishmen to end them. On the 1st June, 1863, he moved in the Municipal Council that it be a recommendation of that Council that all Irishmen should combine in some well-devised effort to put an end to a system of spoliation which was rapidly converting this fair and fruitful and once populous country into a desert. The Report on Public Expenditure ultimately drawn up is a model of accurate research, argument, and deduction. It was entirely his inspiration and work, and entitles him not alone to the gratitude of his countrymen, but also to a foremost place amongst political economists. There is a remarkable coincidence between some of its conclusions and the findings of the Royal Commission of 1894. Finally, it supplied Irishmen with ample materials on which to base an unanswerable case for redress.

CHAPTER VII.

A.D. 1863.

THE CORPORATION OF DUBLIN ON THE PUBLIC ACCOUNTS OF GREAT BRITAIN AND IRELAND.

AT a meeting of the Municipal Council of Dublin, held on Tuesday, 21st April, 1863, Alderman Atkinson, *locum tenens*, in the chair, it was moved by Councillor Dillon, and seconded by Alderman John Reynolds, and carried unanimously :—

That a special committee be appointed to inquire and report to the Council as to the state of the public accounts between Ireland and Great Britain.

On the motion of Councillor Dillon, seconded by Councillor Draper, the following members were appointed to form the Committee :—The Lord Mayor, Alderman J.

Reynolds, Alderman Martin, Councillors Knox, Gray, Martin, Draper, M'Swiney, Byrne, Sullivan, and Dillon. The Committee elected Councillor John Blake Dillon chairman. The Report contains the following :—

"Your Committee deemed they would most effectually carry out the views of the Council by inviting the co-operation of gentlemen whose names had been prominently before the public in connection with the subject of international finance. With that view they communicated with Mr. Staunton, the Collector-General of Dublin, and with Mr. Fisher of Waterford, each of whom had laboured with laudable energy to diffuse information on the subject. Both these gentlemen promptly responded to the invitation of your Committee, and have given evidence. Your Committee, understanding that Mr. Delahunty of Waterford held views adverse to those of Mr. Fisher and Mr. Staunton, and being desirous that the Council should, as far as possible, be made acquainted with all that could be said on either side of this important question, invited Mr. Delahunty also to communicate his views. He kindly consented to afford the Committee the benefit of his information." These gentlemen were examined by the Committee, and their evidence is printed as an Appendix to the Report.

The Committee proposed for inquiry the following six questions, the comprehensiveness and exhaustive character of which cannot be too highly commended :—

(1) Was the financial arrangement embodied in the 7th Article of the Act of Union just towards Ireland ?

(2) Assuming that arrangement to be just, were its terms fulfilled or violated by the Act 56 George III, which consolidated the two Exchequers ?

(3) Is the actual taxation of Ireland excessive or otherwise, as compared with the taxation of Great Britain and other countries, and with its own resources,

and having regard to the past financial transactions between Great Britain and Ireland?

(4) To what extent are the taxes raised in Ireland expended in Ireland?

(5) How has Ireland (as compared with Great Britain) been treated by the Imperial Legislature in the remission and imposition of taxes?

The Committee made a minute and careful examination of all the points raised in the questions, which is fully set out in the Report, and answered them as follows :—

The first :— in the negative.

The second :—That the financial arrangement of the Union, unjust though it was towards Ireland, was violated to Ireland's detriment by the Act which consolidated the two Exchequers in 1817.

The third :—That the present taxation of Ireland is excessive, as compared with that of Great Britain and other countries, and greater than the past transactions of Great Britain and Ireland, or a due regard to the extent of its present resources, would warrant.

The fourth :—That, of the entire revenue raised in Ireland, the portion annually expended in England or elsewhere out of Ireland amounts to about £4,000,000.

The fifth:—That at the close of the war of 1816 the first important reduction of taxation took place, and we find in that year a repeal of taxes to the amount of £17,196,324, the benefit of which Ireland shared to the extent of £163,155, being less than one per cent. (Return, 1843, No. 573.) From the period last mentioned to the year 1842, inclusive, the Return just referred to shows a total reduction of taxes amounting to £47,966,664, which was apportioned between the two countries as follows :—

Taxes repealed in Great Britain,   £45,549,683
Do.   in Ireland,   ...   2,416,981

In more recent years the imposition, in quick succession, of the income tax, of increased stamp duties, of
increased spirit duties, has helped to swell the annual
remittances to England, and consequently to aggravate
the depression of our industry and the distress of our
people.

The Report proceeds :—

" In entering upon some of the discussions contained
in this Report, your Committee have felt they might
be open to the observation that these questions no
longer possessed any present interest—that they belong
to a past generation, and, having been closed by lapse
of time, cannot now be re-opened. Your Committee,
however, venture to hope that a more accurate knowledge of the financial transactions of the past generation
may have the effect of preventing future financial
injustice, and of silencing an assertion by which every
application for aid in effecting public improvements,
emanating from Ireland, is met in the House of
Commons and by the English press—the assertion
that Ireland has always been, and still is, an expense
and a burden to Great Britain. If it were more generally understood that Ireland has, in times past,
contributed more than her due share of the public
burdens, and that she is still paying more than a fair
proportion, and, finally, that of the large revenue which
is raised in Ireland not one-half is expended at home,
we should be less frequently accused of endeavouring to
relieve Irish distress and subsidizing Irish enterprise
with 'English money.' Ireland owes no debt to
Britain, and she has a right, which every country has, to
have her own money mainly spent within her own
borders. This, at least, is a question the present
practical importance of which will hardly be questioned.
And your Committee are of opinion that the Council
would establish a claim to the lasting gratitude of the

country if, inviting the co-operation of other representative bodies throughout Ireland, they would initiate a
combined effort to obtain some compensation for past
and present financial injustice by a diminution of
existing taxation, and by the expenditure on works of
public improvement in Ireland of a fair proportion
of those taxes which are now annually remitted to
England."

CHAPTER VIII.

A.D. 1862-63-64.

JOSEPH FISHER.

JOSEPH FISHER, born in Youghal in 1816, was a
member of the Society of Friends. The Fishers were
well known and esteemed in Youghal, and always took
a foremost part in any work which had for its object the
amelioration of the social and material condition of
the people. He was educated at the Friends' School,
Newtown, Waterford ; was elected a guardian of the
poor for Youghal Union in 1848 ; and removed to
Waterford in 1854, when he became editor and proprietor of *The Waterford Mail*. Discussion was general
in Ireland about 1862 as to the cause of the very
apparent decline and decay of the country, and
the Chamber of Commerce of Waterford requested
Mr. Fisher to prepare a case for counsel as to the legal
rights of the Irish people under the Treaty of Union.
The work thus commenced grew into his book, *The Case
of Ireland*, which, at the time it was published, was the
ablest impeachment of the fiscal policy pursued by
England towards Ireland since the Union. In a series
of letters addressed to Lord Carlisle, the Whig Viceroy
of Ireland, he stated his conviction that the system of
taxation imposed by the Whigs was the principal cause

of the ruin of the country. His writings reveal him to have been a man of great sympathy, zeal, ability, and earnestness. He played no inconsiderable part in directing the attention of the Irish people in 1863-64 to the question of taxation.

On the 16th March, 1864, Mr. J. B. Dillon, in addressing the Corporation of Dublin, said of him :—

> Mr. Fisher has given us, in his *Case of Ireland*, a book which, without vouching the accuracy of all its conclusions, I am not afraid to characterize as a work exhibiting great ability and great research, and which, emanating from a Conservative and a Protestant, by its tone of manly patriotism recalls the days of Molyneux and Swift.

From the office of *The Waterford Mail*, on 13th January, 1863, he issued a letter to the people of Ireland on the excessive taxation of the country.

Mr. Fisher expressed the following views :—

The capital of Ireland decreased from 1859 to 1862 by over eight millions—that is, by *one-tenth* of the entire capital. The excessive and most unfair taxation which had been placed upon the country must be reckoned the most striking cause of this decrease.

The drain of Irish capital was in defiance of the principles which guided the statesmen who framed the Act of Union. Those principles were based on a proposition so simple and so rational, that the meanest mind could appreciate its import—namely, that the two islands, Great Britain and Ireland, should contribute to the imperial revenue in proportion to their respective means. In 1862 the annual income of Ireland assessed for income tax was £22,746,344, and the income of the United Kingdom £301,345,867. The Irish income was *one-fourteenth* of the whole.

Mr. Gladstone came into office in 1853, and during his career loaded Ireland with taxes. He imposed the property and income tax upon lands and income ;

he burdened trade and commerce with stamp duties ; he loaded property with legacy duties ; he increased the excise by nearly doubling the spirit duties. During the five years ending 1862, the amount which the published returns admitted was raised by taxes in Ireland was £33,583,332, that is, £14,294,017 over what Sir Robert Peel received in the five years from 1841 to 1846. And instead of this being in the proportion of *one to fourteen*, as it ought to have been, it was as *one to ten*. This was a very great injustice.

The relative amounts which had been raised by taxation in Great Britain and Ireland, and the great increase which had taken place in the amount which Ireland had paid, deserved attention. Not only had Ireland been very heavily taxed within the past seven years, but also the proportion which her contribution bore to that of the empire had been seriously increased.

The Irish revenue returns stated our payments in the five years ending 1862 had been £33,500,000, but they did not include the receipts of the Irish Post Office, which had been over £1,000,000 ; they did not include the receipts from Crown Lands in Ireland, which had been nearly £250,000 ; nor did they include customs paid in England on goods consumed in Ireland. If these items had been added, it would have made the Irish payments to the revenue in the five years ending 1862 at least £36,000,000, and those of Great Britain £303,000,000 ; or, in other words, the annual average payments from Great Britain had been £60,600,000, and from Ireland £7,200,000.

The equitable mode of adjustment would be that each country should contribute in proportion to its income ; nay, that very principle was affirmed in the income tax itself, for the income of £200 a year paid the same poundage as that of £20,000. But when this

principle was applied to Irish taxation, the grievous
wrong inflicted on Ireland was evident, and was made
plain in the following simple manner:—The annual
income of Great Britain was £278,599,525, and her
annual average taxation £60,600,000, or *at the rate
of four shillings and sixpence in the pound.* The annual
income of Ireland was £22,746,344, and her average
annual taxation £7,200,000, or *at the rate of six shillings
and sixpence in the pound;* so that Ireland was paying
to the imperial revenue at the rate of two shillings in
the pound on her income more than Great Britain.
This was not, and could not be, just to Ireland.

Ireland had, during the five years ending 1862, contributed to the Imperial Exchequer £2,000,000 a year
more than her fair proportion ; and that was one of the
causes, if not the principal cause, of her depression.

Money raised as poor rate was spent in the country;
the amount raised as income tax was spent out of the
country. Everyone who paid income tax had so much
less to spend at home ; and therefore the tradesman
and artisan suffered, trade and commerce languished,
and the country showed retrogression.

It was for the people of Ireland to say if they thought
the great increase of taxation was right, just, and proper.

He appealed to the Irish people on January, 1863:—

Now for the remedy. If you think with me that Ireland is too
heavily taxed, that she is drained of that capital which ought to
be used to improve her system of tillage, to extend her trade and
commerce, and to employ her people, you have legal and constitutional means of explaining your grievances and of asking for
redress ; and the present juncture is particularly favourable. The
Chancellor of the Exchequer has a large balance to his credit, as
the revenue of last year exceeded the previous one. The property
and income tax was, last session, continued only for a year, and the
whole financial system of the empire must undergo revision. If
you are satisfied with your condition—if you believe that Ireland
is prosperous—if you consider she is fairly taxed, you have merely
to sit still and do nothing. Should you decide on this course,

and if any of your representatives try and obtain "justice for Ireland," the finance minister will quietly put him down by saying, "The people of Ireland are satisfied with their condition." But if you feel with me that you have been unfairly taxed, and that our common country has been injured thereby, you are bound by the claims of that country, you are urged by dictates of justice and right, to adopt every legal and constitutional way of expressing your opinions. I believe, in so doing, you will have the sympathy and support of a large section of the English people, who have, I am confident, no wish to save their own pockets at your expense ; and who, if you represent your case to them, will not only admit the injury which has been done to you, but will aid you in obtaining redress. You will have the support of the large landed proprietors and great commercial interests of your own country, who, lest the imputation of selfishness should have been imputed to them, have heretofore refrained from stating the grievances they suffered. It rests with you, the Irish people, to make a vigorous and combined effort to raise your country from the slough into which she has fallen. If you are calm, resolute, temperate, and combined—if you will resort to those means which are legal and constitutional of expressing your grievances—you may (and I fervently hope you will) succeed in bringing back to Ireland the sunshine of prosperity, and see her flourish under a more equitable system of taxation. If my feeble efforts but evoke in your bosoms the desire to improve the condition of Ireland, and to remove the incubus which presses upon her, I shall feel—what must to any of her sons be the highest reward—that I have tried at least to promote the prosperity of my native country.

On the 23rd January, 1863, he again addressed the people of Ireland :—

Were Ireland in a really prosperous condition—were her crops increasing, her land more productive, her flocks and herds becoming more numerous—were her people employed and contented—were pauperism and crime declining—were her exports in excess of her imports, and her investments gradually becoming greater—I should most gladly rejoice in her prosperity ; and in this happy state of affairs, I would not be disposed to press too far the question of unfair taxation, which has so greatly injured us ; but when I see that Ireland is depressed, partly from the ungenial seasons with which it has pleased God to visit us, and partly from the effects of what seems to me to be vicious legislation ; and when I find that our taxation exceeds by more than fifty per cent. the proportion which either in equity, by a comparison of our means, or by contract under that treaty which called the Parliament of the United Kingdom into existence, I cannot refrain from lifting my voice and using my pen (feeble though their utterance may be) to obtain for Ireland that relief from taxation to which she is, by equity and by contract alike, entitled.

In Letter XV of *The Case of Ireland*, published in London, September, 1863, he wrote :—

The question of taxation is neither a party nor a sectarian question ; it is, in the broadest significance of the word, an Irish question. I have endeavoured to treat it in the same spirit, and having laid the case of Ireland before you, the Irish people, it remains for you to act thereupon in a way which will secure to you and your children the rights to which by justice, as well as by agreement and contract, you are entitled. You should press your case upon the attention of Parliament—you should call upon your representatives to demand the adjustment of the public burdens in such a way as to relieve Ireland from undue taxation. You should make the question essentially a national one, and pursue it with vigour and determination until you accomplish your object, and you will find your reward in the advancement of your native land. If I can aid the Irish people in any well-directed effort to bring back to our country that prosperity which she has once enjoyed, and to which she is so fully entitled, I shall feel that I am only discharging the duty which every Irishman owes to his native land.

The concluding letter (XVI), September, 1863, contained :—

The DEBT with which Ireland has been charged is *illegal.*
The TAXATION with which Ireland has been loaded is *illegal.*
The BURDENS which have been laid on her shoulders are *illegal.*

I therefore urge my fellow-countrymen of all classes, creeds, and professions, to unite in endeavouring to get rid of the excessive taxation which has been placed upon Ireland. I call them to union on behalf of their country. They have right and justice, truth and equity, on their side ; and if they will calmly, peacefully, and unitedly stand for the cause of Ireland, whose case I lay before the whole world, they will find that those eternal principles of justice, which are immutable, must prevail—that an end must come to the wrong and injustice that has been inflicted upon this country.

No more strenuous protest was made against the over-taxation of Ireland than that of the patriot Quaker of Youghal, no more zealous worker aroused public opinion on the question, no more tactful leader sought the union of the people for the attainment of practical results, no more critical witness grappled as successfully with the Treasury officials and their bewildering arrays of statistics before the Select Committee of 1864. Thirty-three years have passed, and the eternal, immutable principles of justice, which he believed would soon prevail, still fail to regulate the financial affairs of Ireland. Be it not said that he has written in vain. His appeal of 1863 was re-echoed from a hundred Irish platforms in 1896-97.

CHAPTER IX.

A.D. 1863-64.

AGITATION AND ORGANIZATION.

AT a banquet in New Ross on 7th October, 1863, the toast of

The re-adjustment of the taxation of Ireland

was given and spoken to.

At a special meeting of the Dublin Corporation on Tuesday, the 27th October, 1863, the report of the Select Committee on the Public Accounts of Great Britain and Ireland was unanimously adopted, and it was ordered that 500 copies be printed and circulated amongst Members of Parliament and Irish public bodies.

The Nation thus commented on the unanimous adoption of the report :—

But the work they have done is of immense value. They have placed on record an authentic statement of an undeniable grievance, which presses on all Irishmen, without distinction of class or creed, and from which the whole country should demand to be relieved. We hope the other corporations of Ireland will take up the question, and not only these, but also the boards of guardians, the town commissioners, the chambers of commerce, and, in short, societies of all sorts. Ample ground for a strong national movement of all creeds and parties against the flagrant injustice of our taxation is furnished by the admirable report which now has the sanction and authorization, by unanimous vote, of the Dublin Corporation.

The review of Mr. Fisher's book which appeared in *The Cork Examiner* was written by O'Neill Daunt, and called forth a letter from Mr. Robert Longfield, Q.C., M.P., in October, 1863, in which he stated that the taxation of Ireland was recently duplicated, and that the country was groaning with the grievous oppression of excessive taxation, and he thus replied to the appeal for united action on this question :—

I quite agree with you in thinking how very desirable it would be if we could effect anything like a concurrence of action, or even of opinion, on this subject in our 105 members ; but I do not forget that on Colonel Dunne's motion this year connected with the taxation of Ireland there were scarcely forty members in the House.

O'Neill Daunt, in reply, said :—

The subject of Colonel Dunne's motion is far too important, and the wrong inflicted on Ireland is too susceptible of proof, to be suffered to pass into oblivion.

On Monday, the 14th December, 1863, a public meeting, convened by requisition

For the purpose of considering what steps should be taken to procure a reduction in the taxation of Ireland,

was held in Waterford. The chair was taken by the
Mayor, and there were also present the High Sheriff,
the President of the Chamber of Commerce, and many
leading citizens. The following resolutions were unanimously adopted :—

(1) That the increase which has taken place in the taxation of
Ireland is highly injurious to her interests ; that she is now taxed
more heavily in proportion to her income than Great Britain ; and
that this disproportional increase in her taxation is contrary to the
Act under which Ireland became an integral portion of the United
Kingdom.

(2) That the excess of taxation absorbs a large portion of the
property of Ireland, and thereby prevents the increase of the funds
which would afford employment to the people, and it has thereby
increased emigration from Ireland, and thus lessened the material
strength of the empire.

(3) That the amount unfairly taxed from this country, to a
return of which we are indisputably entitled, has been demonstrated to exceed two millions per annum, which would more than
suffice for the payment of the grand jury rates, amounting to
£1,088,828 ; the poor rates, amounting to £578,789 ; the medical
charities, £106,858 ; and the total abolition of the income tax,
amounting to £740,500 per annum, to the relief of which it should
be applied.

Finally, the meeting appointed a committee to carry
out its object, form an organization, and prepare a
petition for presentation to Parliament.

The committee thus formed in Waterford went
steadily to work, and in quick succession held public
meetings and formed branch organizations—at Waterford, with the Mayor as chairman ; at Limerick, with
the Mayor as chairman ; at Kilkenny, with the Mayor
as chairman ; at Clonmel, with the Mayor as chairman ;
at Carrick-on-Suir, with a Deputy-Lieutenant as chairman ; at New Ross, with the Chairman of Town Commissioners as chairman ; at Dundalk, with the President
of the Chamber of Commerce as chairman. The following address was circulated throughout Ireland :—

THE REDUCTION OF TAXATION.

Inasmuch as the taxation of Ireland for imperial objects exceeds the amount which this country should pay, either upon a comparison of her income with that of the United Kingdom, or according to the conditions of the Act of Union between Great Britain and Ireland, and inasmuch as this excessive taxation absorbs those funds which would otherwise afford employment to the Irish people, and help to prevent emigration;

It is desirable that an association should be formed, which should use every lawful means to benefit Ireland by obtaining a just reduction in her taxation, or the application of the surplus over her rightful proportion to the diminution of local burdens ; and that all those who contribute to the funds shall constitute the members of this association, which shall be called

The Association for the Reduction of Taxation in Ireland ;

And the executive *pro tem.* consist of the presidents and secretaries of the branch associations which have been or may be formed ; and that the National Bank be treasurers thereto.

On the 8th February, 1864, the text of a petition to Parliament, which set forth the over-taxation of Ireland and claimed redress, was read at a meeting of the Dublin Corporation. Resolutions were adopted at many public boards, of which that of the Limerick Corporation and of the Thurles Board of Guardians, respectively, are here set out :—

Adopted at a meeting of the Corporation of Limerick on 30th January, 1864—

That the best thanks of this Council and of every Irishman are due to the Dublin Corporation for the Report on the State of the Public Accounts between Great Britain and Ireland received this day, and we hereby pledge ourselves to co-operate with them in obtaining from the Imperial Parliament such remedial measures in financial matters as will relieve Ireland from the embarrassments under which she labours.

Adopted at a meeting of the Guardians in February, 1864—

That our marked thanks, as Guardians of the Poor in the Union of Thurles, County Tipperary, are eminently due and are hereby given

to the Municipal Council of Dublin, and in a special manner to the
honest, patriotic, and intelligent chairman of its Special Committee
on the State of the Public Accounts between Great Britain and
Ireland, John Blake Dillon, Esq., for the clear exposure contained
in their report of the wrong inflicted on Ireland by unjust taxation,
and that our clerk transmit to them a copy of this resolution, with
the assurance of our very earnest desire to co-operate with them in
demanding redress.

Such was the state of feeling evoked in Ireland in the
winter of 1863-64. Public opinion was beginning to
recognise that the decay of the country was in great
part really attributable to excessive taxation. When
General Dunne again, on the 26th February, 1864,
asked for an inquiry, he was accorded by the House
of Commons quite a different hearing to that which
had been previously given to him.

- - - - - - - -

CHAPTER X.

A.D. 1864.

THE STATISTICAL AND SOCIAL INQUIRY SOCIETY OF IRELAND.

PROTEST BY LORD MORRIS.

ON Wednesday, the 16th March, 1864, Mr. Joseph J.
Murphy read a paper before the Statistical and Social
Inquiry Society of Ireland on the "Debt and Taxation
of Ireland." It was practically a reply to the "Report
of the Special Committee of the Municipal Council of
Dublin on the State of the Public Accounts between
Ireland and Great Britain." The figures in the Report
were taken as correct, but the inferences drawn by the
Committee were challenged. The accuracy of the statement that Ireland paid as much as it was able to pay
previous to 1853 was denied. Lowering of taxes on

commodities in England, their increase in Ireland, the expenditure of a large proportion of imperial revenue in England, the greater benefits conferred on England by reductions and remissions of taxation, were all jauntily made little of as of no consequence. The finding that the taxation of Ireland is excessive as compared with that of England was described as "a most extraordinary statement." It was admitted that it would be possible to impose nominally equal taxes in such a way as to be really very unequal; but no effort was made to practically apply this salutary rule to the circumstances of Ireland. In conclusion, he avowed his belief that Ireland needed something very different from untaxed incomes for the rich, and cheap whisky for the poor, but wisely abstained from mentioning his panacea. The following quotation will briefly show his fallacious arguments and begging of the question :—

The proof advanced by the Committee for the astounding assertion that we are more heavily taxed by our lighter rates of taxation, is merely that our total taxation is larger than that of Great Britain in proportion to the wealth of the two countries as indicated by the income tax returns. In other words, it is a grievance that the indirect taxes are more productive, in proportion to the income tax, in Ireland than in Great Britain. In no case would this be a grievance unless the taxation were imposed so as to be really unequal. But the high relative productiveness of the indirect taxation of Ireland is in part due to the propensity of our people to prefer spirits, which are heavily taxed, to beer, which is moderately taxed; and the low relative productiveness of the income tax is partly due to the lower average of income in Ireland, which causes fewer of them to come within reach of the tax; partly to the small size of farms in Ireland, which exempts nearly all farmers from the tax; and partly to a favourable difference in the law, which charges the tax on real property and on agricultural tenants by a very moderate official valuation, instead of the actual letting value.

In the discussion which followed the reading of the paper, Mr. Shannon referred to the declining state of

the country as a reason why Ireland should be exempt
from undue pressure of taxation, and expressed the
hope that the present movement, which had been so
well conducted by Mr. Dillon, would produce beneficial
results for the country.

Alderman Dillon begged to make a few observations.
He had not come prepared to make an elaborate reply.
Anything that he said should not be taken as the best
that could be advanced in answer to that gentleman. As
regards the payment of the two-seventeenths, Ireland's
quota fixed by the Treaty of Union, Mr. Murphy urged
that Ireland was unable to pay it, and did not pay it.
Mr. Dillon said that either answer was a good one. If
they did not pay it, it was reasonable to suppose that
they were unable to pay it; and if they were unable
to pay it, it was clear that they should not be called
upon to do so. If it were stipulated that Ireland should
pay two-seventeenths, and she did not pay it, what
other conclusion would he come to than that her
revenue broke down under the weight? He concluded
by expressing his emphatic dissent from the proposition that Ireland should be considered as if she were
an English county.

A most important speech was delivered by Mr.
Michael Morris, Q.C. (now a Law Lord, Lord Morris of
Spiddal). He said that his friend Alderman Dillon,
with his practical patriotism and great ability, had
applied himself to the question of taxation, and had
disposed of a good many of the arguments of the
lecturer as applicable to the taxation of the country at
the time of the Union, and up to the year 1816. He
did not intend to refer to either of those periods, because
he thought than an inquiry referring to those times was
rather of an antiquarian character. The questions which
affected them most were, how the taxes stood at present,
what they were in the year 1864, and where they were

spent. Sydney Smith said that no man was certain of anything in his life but of his death and the taxes he had to pay. Applying this saying to this country, he might say that death and taxes were almost synonymous terms. He should object most strongly to the lecturer's argument that taxes should be put upon what he called pernicious luxuries. The lecturer seemed to have some extraordinary dislike to whisky, and, according to him, it was no matter if five millions of taxes were raised on the commodity, because he considered it pernicious. He was one of those who considered that taxes were raised for the purpose of revenue, and not for the purpose of putting down by an indirect mode any species of industry. He believed that up to the year 1852 Ireland paid her full share of the taxes of the empire; yet they had this startling fact that, from 1852 to the present time, new taxes were put upon this country to an amount which the learned lecturer admitted was £1,750,000. The taxes of this country since 1852 had increased 33 per cent., without an increase of 1 per cent. in England. He was old enough to recollect that even in 1852 there were wise persons who then complained that Ireland was excessively taxed; but even assuming that in 1852 the taxation was reasonable—the taxation since that time having increased 33 per cent.—was there any particular cause for such an increase? Sir Robert Peel, in consequence of the repeal of the Corn Laws, reduced the taxation of this country. Now, what took place since 1847, assuming that up to 1852 Ireland was paying her fair share, that she should be burdened with two millions more of taxation? To use the words of Sydney Smith, he thought a man should be trepanned before he could be convinced of the justice of it. It was said that Scotland and Yorkshire existed, although no taxes were spent there; but was it any argument to say that, because one man was strong enough to bear an injury, every other man should bear it? It was new to him to hear that taxes were not spent in Yorkshire and Scotland ; and it certainly was an extraordinary notion that taxes could be taken out of a country and spent elsewhere without injury to that country. If he met anyone foolish enough to make such an assertion, he would not think it worth his while to answer him. The report of the Committee of the Corporation showed that a large amount of the taxes of the country was spent out of it. Lord Byron said that the Union between this country and England was like the union between the whale and the thing it swallowed. Ireland participated in the payment of taxes, but not in their expenditure. The question which he would suggest to the practical patriots was, Should not the taxation of this country be spent at home? The Irish people should not be treated as milch cows. There was every disposition shown to take those taxes off and spend them elsewhere, so much so that they were now nearly dry cows. He hoped every prudent man, as he considered he was himself, would join his friend Alderman Dillon in his truly patriotic proposal with reference to taxation, and that that proposal would be ventilated far and near. He believed it would take a man better able to deal with figures than the learned lecturer was to prove to this country the contrary of what had been shown by Alderman Dillon.

CHAPTER XI.

A.D. 1864.

MR. GLADSTONE GRANTS AN INQUIRY TO GENERAL DUNNE.

THE discussions at public boards and at public meetings in Ireland in 1863-64, the overwhelming Irish case made out in the publications of Mr. Dillon and Mr. Fisher, and the aroused state of Conservative and popular public opinion in Ireland, had effect on the House of Commons; for when, on the 26th February, 1864, General Dunne again brought forward the motion rejected in 1863, he was listened to by a full and attentive House. He said that a great change had come over public opinion in Ireland. He never knew the attention of her people to be so thoroughly and earnestly directed to the consideration of her material interests—hitherto much neglected—and especially to the amount of taxation imposed on her as compared with the rest of the kingdom. In Dublin a committee appointed to investigate the matter had taken evidence from witnesses on both sides, and had made an extremely clever report very much in accordance with his views. Similar inquiries had also been conducted in Waterford, Clonmel, Limerick, and other towns. He hoped that was the commencement of an agitation in which every Irishman would take part, and which would bring the question fully and fairly before the legislature.

The great difficulty was the paucity of information. The returns were often contradictory, and no clear accounts seemed to have been kept of the different taxes in Ireland. The object of taxation in Ireland was to get from the country as much as could be squeezed

out of her. He rested his case on two grounds—first,
the Treaty of Union; and second, the relative ability of
each country to bear taxation. On both grounds Ireland was entitled to more favourable treatment than she
received. It was not his opinion that the emigration of
the people ought not to form a subject for regret. He
could not help thinking that it must be a loss to any
country to have its population flying from its shores.
Having quoted ample statistics to show the diminished
capacity of the country to sustain heavy burdens, he
turned to the question of taxation, and he found that
in the last decennial period it had increased from
£48,560,000 to £52,893,000. A nobleman who had
spent a great deal of money in Ireland, and who had
lately returned from the West, assured him that until
the present year he had never despaired of the prospects
of the country. He defied any Chancellor of the Exchequer to add a farthing to the taxation of Ireland.
The people were flying from the country, and no more
taxes could be paid. Two returns had been moved for
—one showing the proportion of taxation to population,
and the other the proportion of taxation to property.
The test of population he considered to be by no means
a fair one, if the plan were adopted of dividing the income by the number of inhabitants. This system was
manifestly greatly to the advantage of the rich country
over the poor one; because in the rich country wealth was
much more largely diffused, and in the poor country the
rate of valuation was much lower. Ireland had become
impoverished by a load of taxation. He asked the
House, was there anything unreasonable in a recon-
sideration of the Treaty of Union for the purpose of
ascertaining whether the promises held out by that
Treaty had been fulfilled, and whether, considering the
relative wealth of the two countries, the method of taxation was just and equal. If he had proved that every

species of wealth and industry had been lessened in
Ireland, he thought the House could not refuse an inquiry to ascertain whether the present taxation of
Ireland was not greater than she could bear. The Irish
people had turned their attention to this subject with
the same ardour that they frequently displayed on far
inferior questions. He moved

> For a select committee to consider the taxation of Ireland, and
> how far it is in accordance with the provisions of the Treaty of
> Union, or just in reference to the resources of the country.

Mr. Hennessy seconded the motion.

Sir Edward Grogan stated that the conviction was
strong and general in Ireland that the country was
grossly over-taxed, and that it was entitled to relief.
Lord Dunkellin concurred that Ireland suffered from
over-taxation. Mr. Longfield considered that there
was injury caused by unjust imposition and unwise remission of taxes since 1852.

Mr. Gladstone, who was Chancellor of the Exchequer,
said, that although the Government would not of themselves have proposed the appointment of such a committee, yet, under the circumstances, finding in the
House of Commons a decided desire on the part of Irish
members for the appointment of a committee to inquire
into Irish taxation, they thought it would not be wise to
oppose such an inquiry. He admitted that Ireland bore
her full proportion of all taxes incident on the labouring
population. He admitted and deplored the distress in
Ireland, whether it was due to taxation, emigration, or
deficient harvests. He hoped that it would soon draw
to a close, and that the future career of Ireland would
be one of happiness and prosperity.

Opinion in Ireland considered that, in whatever sense
the Committee on Parliamentary Taxation might ultimately report, General Dunne was well entitled to the

gratitude of his countrymen for the persistent, and so far successful, efforts which he had made to effect a settlement of the much vexed and most intricate question, the fiscal relations between Great Britain and Ireland. When first he entered upon the controversy, there was everything to discourage, and little to sustain, his application for redress ; but his personal popularity did much. He spoke for an hour and three-quarters, and was listened to with patience and attention. Some Irish opinion considered that the true financial case should be one of indemnity, reparation, and restitution to Ireland.

Nothing could possibly exceed the misrepresentation and acerbity with which *The Times* commented on the debate :—

In dealing with the Irish debate of Friday, not only is it necessary to apply a grain of salt, but when that is done the grain of salt is all that remains. We are disposed to be most charitable (*sic*) to the Irish members, but then our charity must be that which covers a multitude of sins, and therefore every word they said.

When it comes to review the recent movement in Ireland, it is flagrantly untruthful :—

Honourable mention was made of the committees which have been sitting in the less busy and prosperous Irish ports and towns for three years, with nothing to do but make out a case of financial depression ; but it was confessed that their reports were contradictory, on a wrong basis, and good for nothing.

No such confession was made. It was simply invented by *The Times*. After the lapse of more than forty years, these reports are worthy of careful study and examination for their accurate survey of history, their correct application of the principles of political economy, and for their correct deductions.

The fierce attack it made on General Dunne, the disgraceful travesty of truth and fact which appeared in its pages, the sharp contrast between its tone and that of the Chancellor of the Exchequer, boded ill for the final result of the inquiry so auspiciously commenced with the unanimous approval of the House of Commons.

——— ———

CHAPTER XII.

A.D. 1864-65.

GENERAL DUNNE'S COMMITTEE,

"The busiest bit of Irish politics just now is Colonel Dunne's Committee to inquire into Irish taxation." — *O'Neill Daunt's Diary.*

ON the 8th March, 1864, the Select Committee granted to General Dunne was appointed. It originally consisted of fourteen members, but on the 9th March one was added, making fifteen. Eight represented Irish constituencies, six English, and one Scotch. In nationality, seven were Irish, seven English, and one Scotch. In politics, eight belonged to the Conservative party, and seven to the Liberal. It held twenty-six sittings. Most exhaustive evidence, both oral and written, was tendered. An account of its members, who they were, and the witnesses they examined, will help towards understanding the character of the report finally adopted.

Sir Edward Grogan, Bart., was Conservative Member for the City of Dublin. He was educated at Trinity College, Dublin, where he took honours. He was called to the Bar in 1840, and entered Parliament in 1841. He was a firm supporter of the Established Church. *He was absent from the division in which General Dunne's Draft Report was rejected.*

Sir Frederick William Heygate, Bart., was Conservative Member for the County of Londonderry. He was an Englishman, born in Kent in 1822. He was educated at Eton and Trinity College, Cambridge. " Though opposed to violent and unnecessary change, he would lend his aid to reform all proved abuses." *He voted for General Dunne's Draft Report.*

Robert Longfield, Q.C., was the Liberal-Conservative Member for Mallow. He graduated with honours at Trinity College, Dublin, was called to the Irish Bar in 1834, admitted a Queen's Counsel in 1852, and first elected to Parliament in 1859. *He voted for General Dunne's Draft Report.*

Mr. John Pope Hennessy, afterwards Knight of Malta and K.C.M.G., was Conservative Member for the King's County. Born in Cork in 1834, he studied at the Queen's College, Cork, entered Parliament in 1859, and was called to the Bar at the Inner Temple in 1861. He was appointed Governor of Labuan in 1867, of the West African Settlements in 1872, of the Bahamas in 1873, of the Windward Islands in 1875, of Hong Kong in 1877, and of the Mauritius in 1882. Here he quarrelled with Mr. Clifford Lloyd, and retired on full pension. *He was absent from the division in which General Dunne's Draft Report was rejected.*

Sir George Conway Colthurst, Bart., was added when Mr. Monsell was discharged. He was Liberal Member for Kinsale, having entered Parliament in 1863. *He voted against General Dunne's Draft Report.*

Lord John Thomas Browne was Liberal Member for Mayo. He was the third son of the second Marquis of Sligo. Born in Westport in 1824, he served in the Royal Navy as midshipman and lieutenant from 1837 to 1850. *He voted for General Dunne's Draft Report.*

The O'Conor Don (Charles Owen) was Liberal Member for Roscommon. Born in Dublin in 1838, and

educated at Bath, he represented Roscommon in
Parliament from 1860 to 1880. Was High Sheriff of
Sligo in 1863, and is now (1897) Her Majesty's Lieutenant and Custos Rotulorum for Roscommon. He is
a Senator of the Royal University of Ireland, a Commissioner of Intermediate Education, and a Privy
Councillor. He was a member of the Royal Commission on the Financial Relations of Great Britain
and Ireland in 1894-5-6, and was elected chairman of
that Commission on the death of Mr. Childers. *He
voted for General Dunne's Draft Report.*

Mr. Banks Stanhope was added when Lord Stanley
was discharged. He was Conservative Member for
North Lincolnshire. *He voted against General Dunne's
Draft Report.*

Sir Stafford Northcote, afterwards Lord Iddesleigh,
was Conservative Member for Stamford. He was born
in London in 1818, educated at Eton and Balliol College, Oxford. Called to the Bar in 1847, he succeeded
his father as eighth baronet in 1851. He was in the
House of Commons from 1855 to 1885, and was raised
to the peerage in the latter year. He was President of
the Board of Trade, Secretary of State for India, Chancellor of the Exchequer, and First Lord of the Treasury.
He died in 1887. He published in 1862 *Twenty Years
of Financial Policy*, at page 214 of which he records that
Mr. Gladstone " ultimately raised the spirit duties to
ten shillings a gallon, or very nearly four times the
duty paid on Irish spirits before 1853." He makes no
remark on the justice or equity of thus quadrupling Irish
taxation. *He voted against General Dunne's Draft
Report, and his report was then adopted instead.*

Mr. Edward Howes was Conservative Member for
East Norfolk. Born in 1813, he was educated at
St. Paul's School and Trinity College, Cambridge,
of which he became a Fellow. First elected in 1859.
He voted against General Dunne's Draft Report.

Mr. Alexander Struthers Finlay was Liberal Member for Argyll. Born in 1806, he was educated at Harrow. First returned to Parliament in 1857. Published in 1864 *Our Monetary System. He was absent from the division in which General Dunne's Draft Report was rejected.*

Sir Robert Peel was Liberal Member for Tamworth. Born in 1822, he was the eldest son of the second baronet of that name, and was educated at Harrow. He filled important diplomatic positions from 1844 to 1856. Was Chief Secretary for Ireland from July, 1861, to November, 1865. *He voted against General Dunne's Draft Report.*

Mr. Robert Lowe was Liberal Member for Colne. Born in 1811, he was educated at Winchester College and University College, Oxford. He went to Australia in 1842, and soon rose to distinction as a lawyer and politician. Having amassed a considerable fortune, he returned to England in 1850, and entered Parliament in 1852 as Member for Kidderminster. He was leader-writer on *The Times*, President of the Board of Trade from 1855 to 1858, Vice-President of the Committee of the Council on Education from 1859 to 1864, Chancellor of the Exchequer from 1868 to 1873, when he resigned. He was raised to the peerage as Viscount Sherbrooke in 1880. He was frequently in conflict with his own party, and proposed a tax of one halfpenny on each box of lucifer matches in 1871. *He voted against General Dunne's Draft Report.*

Mr. Thomson Hankey was Liberal Member for Peterborough. Born in London in 1805, he was a West India merchant and a Director of the Bank of England. *He voted against General Dunne's Draft Report.*

The witnesses examined in 1864 were—Sir Colman Michael O'Loghlen, Bart., Q.C., of the Irish Bar. He was born in 1819, and was educated at Trinity College.

He was in Parliament from 1863 to 1877. His evidence was on the Act of Union and the Act for amalgamation of the two Exchequers. He stated as his opinion that in the financial treatment of Ireland both Acts were broken.

Mr. William George Anderson was principal Clerk in the Finance Branch of the Treasury.

Mr. Henry William Chisholm was Chief Clerk of the Exchequer.

Mr. John Blake Dillon gave evidence on 6th and 10th May, 1864. He ably, thoroughly, and broadly presented the Irish case.

Mr. Joseph Fisher gave evidence on 13th May, 3rd, 7th, and 10th June. He most ably presented the Irish case, examined the Treasury accounts since the Union, and frequently came into sharp conflict with Mr. Chisholm.

Mr. William Donnelly, C.B., head of the department for making out agricultural statistics in Ireland, was examined on 10th June.

The Right Hon. Joseph Napier, Lord Chancellor of Ireland, 1858-59, gave evidence on 14th June, principally on the seventh article of the Act of Union. His evidence was "miserable."—*O'Neill Daunt.*

Mr. Nicholas Philpot Leader, M.P., Conservative Member for Cork, gave evidence on 14th June, principally on the state of County Cork.

Mr. Alexander Lambert, County Treasurer for Mayo, gave evidence on 17th June, principally on the distress in the West of Ireland.

The Rev. Dr. O'Regan, P.P., Kanturk, Co. Cork, gave evidence on 17th June, principally on the marked declension in the condition of the peasantry, and that the depressed condition of the country was attributable to increased taxation.

Mr. John Francis Maguire, M.P., gave evidence on

E

21st June, principally on the decay of foreign trade and shipping at Cork, and on the attenuated expenditure of revenue in Ireland.

Mr. Edward Senior, Poor Law Commissioner for Ireland, gave evidence on 24th June that Ireland had unquestionably gone back since 1842.

Mr. John Stephen Dwyer, of Limerick, gave evidence on the 28th June on the rental and valuation of Ireland, the great decline in its prosperity, and that every industry and every class were oppressed by excessive taxation.

Colonel Knox Gore, Lieutenant of County Sligo, gave evidence on 1st July that the people of Ireland, of all classes, were not in as sound a state as at the time of the Union; and that the drain of income from the country left it in such a state that it was not able to bear taxation which in England would be considered fair; and that the taxation of Ireland with reference to the resources of the country was most inequitable.

The Earl of Leitrim, examined on the 1st July, gave evidence that Ireland had deteriorated in a manner most awful to contemplate; that the principle on which England treated Ireland was beggar her neighbour; that the distress in Ireland was directly traceable to taxation; and that the raising of taxes in Ireland to spend them out of Ireland must be the ruin of everybody carrying on business in Ireland; and it was an act of positive dishonesty to carry on public works in England with Irish money.

Sir Percy Nugent, a resident Irish landlord, gave evidence on 1st July that parts of Ireland were now infinitely worse off than they were before the famine; that he himself sensibly felt the increased taxes.

The papers handed to the Committee in 1864 were principally by Mr. Fisher and Mr. Chisholm, and were exhaustive tables of statistics to support the Irish and English cases respectively.

The witnesses examined in 1865 were—

The Marquis of Clanricarde, who gave evidence on arterial drainage on 17th March.

Mr. Henry Hinckman Barnes, Solicitor to the Public Works Loan Commission, London, gave evidence on the loans made to Ireland.

Mr. Alexander Stewart, Solicitor to the Board of Works in Ireland, gave similar evidence.

Colonel M'Kerlie, Chairman of the Board of Works, gave evidence on the 3rd April on loans and arterial drainage.

Mr. William Andrews gave evidence on 27th April on Irish fisheries.

Mr. James Redmond Barry, Assistant Commissioner of Fisheries in Ireland, gave evidence on 27th April that, generally speaking, the fisheries of Ireland were declining.

In a debate on the state of Ireland, on 24th February, 1865, in the House of Commons, on a motion by Mr. John Pope Hennessy, the subjects of Irish taxation and General Dunne's Committee were introduced by Mr. W. E. Gladstone, who was then Chancellor of the Exchequer. The Irish claim to have the taxation levied in Ireland spent in Ireland he denounced as a principle fraught with every kind of mischief to Ireland. He laid down the general doctrine

That to attempt to regulate the public expenditure on any other principle than that which proceeds upon the plan of taking from the subject the smallest amount sufficient for our purposes, and spending the money so obtained in the manner which will cause it to go farthest in the attainment of the public objects in view, would be to proceed on an erroneous system.

He then pointed out a number of Irish exemptions, alluded to the draft reports of the Committee on Irish Taxation, and, though the labours of the committee had not concluded, expressed his preference for that of Sir Stafford Northcote.

General Dunne replied. He said that he had asserted, first, that for sixty years no fair account had been kept between the two countries, and as a consequence that Ireland had been charged with what she was not chargeable with. By the evidence of the Government officials he had proved that proposition. Second, he had asserted that the accounts of the taxation were not in accordance with the Act of Union. He had proved it. Third, he had asserted that Ireland was not taxed according to her ability to pay taxation. He had proved it. The Irish members did not shrink from having this question discussed. He denied that Ireland was a province of England. Ireland was a kingdom bound by close ties to England, and no man was more anxious than he that those ties should be drawn as close as possible. He agreed with the Chancellor of the Exchequer that the object of taxation ought to be to draw as little as possible from the pockets of the people, and that it was the duty of the Government to administer it with the utmost economy. If that test were applied to Ireland, it failed.

The Government drained Ireland, not of water, but of people and money. He understood the very natural preference of the Chancellor of the Exchequer for Sir Stafford Norhcote's report rather than for those of the Irish members.

The Marquis of Salisbury (then Lord Robert Cecil) intervened in the debate, and urged the Government to contribute toward the restoration of prosperity and happiness in Ireland.

Mr. Lowe admitted that the Irish argument; that the taxation of Ireland was similar to the taxation of England, that Ireland was poor and England was rich, and, therefore, that Ireland should not bear the same taxation as England ; would be a very good argument if taxation were adjusted on a cast-iron principle.

Taxation was regulated according to ability. Ireland would be richer if she paid no taxes; but it appeared impossible to say that it was the incidence of taxation which ground down the Irish people.

Mr. Gladstone's public statement of his preference for Sir Stafford Northcote's draft report, at a time when the decision of the committee was, so to speak, *sub judice*, was most unwarrantable and unjustifiable. It undoubtedly helped to secure its adoption, and thereby perpetuated the burden of over-taxation on Ireland.

CHAPTER XIII.

A.D. 1865.

REPORT OF GENERAL DUNNE'S COMMITTEE.

AN ample case was laid before the Committee, even more than sufficient on which to base clear and definite conclusions. General Dunne was chairman, and presided over the meetings with tact and ability. Rarely has the spectacle been witnessed of an Irish soldier directing the deliberations of a committee of expert English financiers, two of whom were afterwards to attain to front rank as Chancellors of the Exchequer. General Dunne was unwearied in his exertions, was in the chair at every meeting, and took a leading part in the examination of witnesses. The Irish case was well presented. Mr. Dillon and Mr. Fisher ably challenged the manner in which the financial provisions of the Treaty of Union had been carried out, and overwhelming evidence of the decay of the country and its diminished ability to bear taxation was given by them and other witnesses. Towards the close of the session of 1864 three draft reports were submitted, one by

General Dunne, the second by the O'Conor Don, and the third by Sir Stafford Northcote. No final decision was arrived at in 1864, on account of the late period of the session when they were presented. On the re-appointment of the Committee in 1865 an additional reference was added, which necessitated the taking of more evidence, and the recasting of the draft reports—

To inquire into the system upon which advances are made and repayments required by the Imperial Government for drainage and other works of public utility in Ireland.

The particular nature of this reference would seem to show that the Treasury officials were not satisfied that the inquiry was tending in England's favour. On the 18th May, when the Committee met to consider their final report, they first, by a majority of ten to one, rejected the following resolutions proposed by Mr. Longfield :—

1st.—That from the length of time which has elapsed since the Union of Great Britain and Ireland, and the complexity of the accounts relative to the taxation of the two countries, it is impossible for the Committee now to say, with any degree of certainty, whether the present taxation of Ireland is, or is not, in accordance with the Articles of Union.

2nd.—That the taxation of Ireland has been greatly increased since 1852, while the taxation of Great Britain has been proportionally diminished, and the present taxation of Ireland is oppressive and unjust with reference to the resources of the country.

3rd.—That there should be afforded by the legislature, from imperial resources, greater facilities than now exist for useful and remunerative expenditure in Ireland to develop her resources.

They then proceeded to consider General Dunne's draft report. The gallant soldier and incorruptible politician had come to clear, precise conclusions on the issues submitted, as the following paragraphs will show :—

(20) Your Committee, therefore, cannot entertain a doubt that during this period [1817-1853] the taxation of Ireland was not in

accordance with the provisions of the Treaty of Union, nor just in reference to the resources of the country, and so far replies to the inquiries referred to it.

(34) Without further pursuing these details, your Committee refers to your consideration the evidence given of the decline in Ireland of almost all kinds of commercial and manufacturing property, and submits that it clearly shows that Ireland has become less able to bear excessive taxation.

(60) The amount which is chargeable for income tax in England £276,119,814, and in Ireland it is £23,014,594. Thus it shows a poundage rate of 4s. 0¾d. in England, and of 6s. 3½d. in Ireland, for imperial taxation on the valuations given by the Government returns ; and in our local taxation of 2s. 3½d. in the pound for England, and 5s. 7¼d. in the pound for Ireland. With such evidence before it, your Committee can come to no other conclusion than that the present taxation of Ireland is oppressive and unjust with reference to the resources of the country.

The evidence received by the Committee more than amply justified these conclusions, and the Report of the Royal Commission of 1894 shows that they were moderate and just. When the draft report was submitted to the Committee, there voted *four* for, and *seven* against. The following table shows how the voting went :—

AYES :

      SIR FREDERICK HEYGATE (*an Englishman representing an Irish constituency.*)

MR. LONGFIELD	...	...	... (*Irish*).
LORD JOHN BROWNE		...	... (*Irish*).
THE O'CONOR DON		...	... (*Irish*).

NOES :

SIR STAFFORD NORTHCOTE	...		... (*English*).
MR. HOWES	...	...	... (*English*).
SIR ROBERT PEEL	...	...	... (*English*).
MR. LOWE	...	...	... (*English*).
MR. HANKEY	...	...	... (*English*).
MR. BANKS STANHOPE		...	... (*English*).
SIR GEORGE COLTHURST		...	... (*Irish*).

ABSENT FROM THE DIVISION :

MR. HENNESSY	...	...	(*Irish*).
SIR EDWARD GROGAN		...	(*Irish*).
MR. FINLAY			(*Scotch*).

The Irish Parliamentary representatives were a majority of the Committee, and if they had done their duty to their country, it is not too much to say that, Ireland might have been spared much of the financial oppression of the past thirty years. All the English members were present, and voted against General Dunne's report. Immediately after the division was taken, he left the chair, and took no further part in the Committee's subsequent proceedings. All his energy and devotion, all his years of labour and unwearied application, were in vain. The cup of success was dashed from his lips at the final moment owing to the defection of one Irish member and the abstention of two. True to the last, he refused to sign the majority report.

Sir Stafford Northcote's report was then adopted, with some amendments. Its general nature may be gathered from the following paragraphs :—

It is not surprising that the large increase which your Committee have noticed in the general taxation between 1852 and 1862, and again in the local taxation since 1845, should have given rise to complaint. Nor is it surprising that louder complaints should have been made in Ireland than by other parts of the United Kingdom. The pressure of taxation will be felt most by the weakest parts of the community ; and as the average wealth of the Irish taxpayers is less than the average wealth of the English taxpayers, the ability of Ireland to bear heavy taxation is evidently less than the ability of England. Mr. Senior, whose evidence upon the position of Ireland will be found very suggestive, remarks that the taxation of England is both the heaviest and lightest of Europe, the heaviest as regards the amount raised, the lightest as regards the ability to bear that amount ; but that in the case of Ireland it is heavy both as regards the amount and as regards the ability of the contributor ; and he adds that England is the most lightly taxed, and Ireland the most heavily taxed, country in Europe, though both are nominally liable to equal taxation.

If Ireland were to be relieved of two or three millions of taxation on the ground of her poverty, and those two or three millions had to be made up by an addition to the taxation of

England, the burdens of the poorer districts of Great Britain would
actually be increased for the purpose of diminishing the burdens,
not only of the poorest, but also of the richest, districts of
Ireland.

It admitted that there had been departures from
the terms of the Treaty of Union, strictly interpreted
—that the recent levelling up of taxation in Ireland
had caused complaint.   It indicated tests of the comparative ability of the two countries, but did not push
the investigation to its logical conclusion.   It admitted
that Ireland had recently suffered, but denied that it
was owing to the pressure of taxation.   Expenditure
on such works as naval arsenals must be regarded from
a national point of view.   Mr. Lowe strongly insisted
on the principle of "*individual taxation.*"   Nevertheless,
the reason advanced by the Committee for declining
to recommend a reduction of Irish burdens was that
the burdens of "*the poorer districts of Great Britain*"
would be thereby increased.

O'Neill Daunt, in a letter of the 3rd June, 1865,
addressed to the Secretary of the National League,
epitomized the majority Report :—

Its omission of cardinal facts ; its fallacious reasoning on facts
isolated from others which are essential to their due consideration ;
the candour with which our leading statements are confessed to be
true ; the absence of all notion that we are entitled to any redress
. . . . Colonel Dunne and his allies are entitled to our hearty
thanks for what they have effected.

Sir Edward Hamilton described the report as
"somewhat impotent." Irish opinion characterized it
as a palpable evasion of the issues submitted, and
as clearly showing that in money matters England was
unwilling to treat Ireland fairly and honourably. No
action was taken on it, and it remains to this day a
dead letter.

CHAPTER XIV.

A.D. 1865.

" THE DUBLIN UNIVERSITY MAGAZINE."

The Dublin University Magazine for April, 1865, had the following remarks on Irish taxation :—

" Close thinkers will not forget that important remissions of indirect taxation have been made from time to time since modern financial principles were established by the introduction of Free Trade, which have been arranged with especial regard to the development of particular manufactures and branches of commerce that were purely English interests. By those remissions Ireland received injury, being visited as a consequence with an augmented income tax and an increase of indirect taxes, as in the case of the excessive duty on spirits, resulting in the shutting up of distilleries and the annihilation of the employment of large numbers of workmen."

It then quoted with approval the following views of Lord Dunkellin :—

He maintained that the imposition of the income tax on Ireland was unfair towards that country. When the late Sir Robert Peel imposed the tax on England in 1842, he did not extend it to Ireland, but he subjected her to two other additional burdens which he regarded as an equivalent for that exemption. He laid on a duty of 1s. per gallon on spirits manufactured in Ireland, and he also raised her stamp duties to the same level as the English stamp duties. Well, how did matters stand with Ireland in 1865 ? Why, when Sir R. Peel placed the extra shilling on Irish spirits, the tax was augmented to only 3s. 8d. per gallon, and since then the Irish spirit duty has been doubled. The increased stamp duty also remained; and, in addition to that, they had been burdened with the income tax itself, which they were forced to pay before they got their income. That was the state of things under which they had the grim satisfaction of being congratulated by the

Chancellor of the Exchequer on their immunity from taxation. The tendency of their financial policy had been to destroy rather than to stimulate the industry of Ireland.

The article then continued :—" What is complained of is, that in the arrangement of taxation English interests alone are regarded, and that the effect is to throw an undue proportion of the public burdens upon Ireland. Suppose it be asked that the Chancellor of the Exchequer, in framing his next budget, should consider what remissions or re-adjustment of taxation he can devise which would have the effect of extending any important department of Irish enterprise, will Mr. Lowe give him support ? If he desire to act with perfect fairness, he ought ; but, instead of being guided by equity, he is found declaring that ' it is not the incidence of taxation that has ground down the Irish people.' Has it been for their benefit that special taxes have crushed important industries ? "

CHAPTER XV.

A.D. 1865.

THE O'CONOR DON ON THE EVIDENCE RECEIVED BY THE IRISH TAXATION COMMITTEE.

THE discussions in the *English* and *Irish* press on the report of General Dunne's Committee, the controversies on matters of fact and principle which it evoked, and the contradictory opinions to which it gave rise, caused the O'Conor Don to publish an examination of the evidence. He treated it calmly and dispassionately, made no effort to strain after effect, weighed the arguments advanced on both sides with judicial impartiality, and adduced temperate and logical conclusions. Nevertheless, the studied moderation of his examination

made his conclusions not only persuasively convincing,
but also a most formidable indictment of English fiscal
policy towards Ireland. He pointed out that similar
taxation imposed on peoples differing in habits, wants,
commerce, and manufactures could not produce similar
results ; that Irish opinion was convinced that the
Act of Union placed an unjust burden on Ireland, and
that its provisions had been fraudulently carried out.
He enunciated the doctrine that—

Equality of taxation in no way depends on similarity in the
actual taxes ;

and that since 1853, whilst the balance of remission
was in favour of England, the balance on the side of
taxes imposed was on the side of Ireland. An examination of taxation statistics for the period from 1852 to
1862 disclosed results to which must be attributed the
general outcry in Ireland of late years respecting taxation. A discussion was idle which urged a difference
between the taxes on a country and those on the
individuals who lived in it. Indirect taxes, levied on
wants and not on means, unquestionably pressed more
heavily on some classes of individuals than on others.
He replied to the *individual taxation* argument by
stating that, theorize as we might, there was more than
a geographical distinction between Great Britain and
Ireland—the difference between them was as great as
between nations at different extremities of the globe.
He concluded with the statement that, if contribution in
proportion to resources was in force, Ireland would
have a strong claim for a remission of taxation. His
summarized conclusions are here set out *in extenso :*—

1st.—That in the Act of Union the principle of payments
towards the general expenditure proportionate to the resources of
the two countries was clearly recognised.

2nd.—That it was so recognised and laid down at the basis of the Union, because at that time the liabilities of the two countries in the way of national debt were not considered to be respectively proportionate to their resources, the debt of Ireland being comparatively lower than the debt of Great Britain.

3rd.—That the contributions of each towards the general expenditure were settled in the proportion of two for Ireland and fifteen for Great Britain, this being the estimate then made of the relative resources of the two countries.

4th.—That at the time of the Union a reduction in taxation and a diminution in debt, through the instrumentality of the sinking fund, were apparently confidently expected, and the heavy charges consequent on the great European war seem not to have been anticipated.

5th.—That these heavy charges were to a great extent instrumental in falsifying the expectations of the framers of the Union, and that under these Ireland completely broke down, not being able to meet by revenue the amount of her proportion of contribution, partly from the fact of her not reaping the same collateral advantages from the war as Great Britain, and partly also because the proportion was, perhaps, originally too great.

6th.—That during the continuance of the war the taxation of Great Britain increased more than 100 per cent., and her debt nearly 70 per cent. ; whilst, with an almost similar increase in her taxation, the debt of Ireland has been quadrupled, this undue increase in her debt arising from the fact that she failed to raise by revenue as great a proportion of her contribution as was raised by Great Britain.

7th.—That in consequence of this failure she lost the advantage which in 1800 she possessed, and at the end of the war was subject to a larger proportionate debt than Great Britain.

8th.—That this result having taken place, the exchequers were amalgamated, and all distinctions arising out of the proportionate contribution of revenue were done away with, one general financial system for the United Kingdom being established, although under it exact similarity in taxes was not adopted.

9th.—That since the amalgamation of the exchequers taxes have been repealed to the amount of £77,968,829, and taxes imposed to the amount of £40,710,862, leaving a balance of remissions of £37,257,967 ; but of this balance Ireland enjoyed only 1·36 per cent., and Great Britain 98·64 per cent.

10th.—That through these remissions the trade, commerce, and prosperity of the United Kingdom have largely advanced ; but that

in those benefits Ireland has not participated to the same extent as
Great Britain, probably in consequence of her comparative want of
trade and manufactures.

11th.—That during the last ten years a large increase in the
taxation of the kingdom had taken place; but the increase had
been proportionately greater in Ireland than in Great Britain,
the increase in Ireland having been since 1855, 52 per cent., and in
Great Britain only 17 per cent.

12th.—That during the same period the increase in the wealth
of the two countries, as estimated by the returns to the income tax,
was 10 per cent. for Ireland, and 21 per cent. for Great Britain.

13th.—That thus, whilst there has been an absolute increase in
the taxation of Great Britain, there has been a comparative decrease, the advance in her resources being at a more rapid rate
than the advance in her taxation ; but that in Ireland there has
been both a comparative and absolute increase in taxation, the advance in wealth being there in a lower ratio than the advance in
taxation.

14th.—That these contrary results from a similar system of
taxation seem chiefly to be due to the extraordinary elasticity of
British resources, and to the great development which her trade
receives on the reduction of taxes affecting it—an elasticity and
development not enjoyed in Ireland.

15th.—That at the present day Ireland is subject to no tax from
which Great Britain is free ; but Great Britain is subject to certain
imposts, making a revenue of about £4,000,000, from which Ireland is exempt ; but that it does not appear that, were these imposts extended to Ireland, they would yield a considerable amount
of revenue.

16th.—That under this system of almost identical taxation
Ireland contributes about 10 per cent. of the general revenue,
whilst her wealth, as tested by the income tax returns and other
data, does not appear to be more than 7 per cent.

17th.—That of the entire revenue of Great Britain, 59·9 per
cent. is contributed by taxes on articles of general consumption,
which in the main are taxes on population, and 21·8 per cent. by
direct taxes, or taxes on wealth ; but of the revenue of Ireland,
75 per cent. is contributed by taxes on articles of consumption, and
only 14 per cent. by taxes on wealth.

18th.—That, with the exception of the tax on spirits, there does
not appear to be any tax pressing peculiarly on any branch of Irish
industry, and the comparative greater heaviness of taxation in that

country appears to be due to the comparative poverty of its inhabitants.

19th.—That the local taxation of Ireland, as far as such can be ascertained, bears a still greater proportion to that of Great Britain than the imperial taxation of the one country does to that of the other, the proportions of local taxation being 11·7 per cent. to 88·3 per cent., whilst imperial taxation, as above stated, is contributed in the proportion of 10 per cent. to 90 per cent.

20th.—That as regards grants in aid of local taxation, including in them the grant for the Irish Constabulary, the proportion received by Ireland is considerable, but is now lower than before the repeal of the Corn Laws, many grants having been since made to Great Britain in consideration of the supposed injury done to the landed interest through the abolition of protection.

21st.—That on this ground, also, the payment of the entire expense of the Irish Constabulary was placed on the Consolidated Fund, notwithstanding which the proportion now received by Ireland is smaller than before, although it cannot be said that she derived more benefit than Great Britain from the establishment of Free Trade.

22nd.—That at various times sums have been set aside for grants or advances for works of public utility, and, as a rule, it does not appear that any loss to the State has arisen from this practice, although at some exceptional periods, such as that of the Irish famine, sums were advanced the repayment of which had to be remitted.

23rd.—That under the Land Improvement Acts £1,804,467 has been advanced in Ireland, none of which has been remitted ; that of this £1,460,178, principal and interest, has been repaid, and the rest is in regular course of repayment.

24th.—Finally, that in all these grants and advances Ireland seems to have fairly participated ; and that, according to the reports of the Commissioners of Public Works, she seems to have been greatly served by them.

CHAPTER   XVI.

A.D. 1866-67-68.

SIR JOSEPH N. M'KENNA.

IN an address to his constituents at Youghal, on the
21st September, 1866, Sir Joseph N. M'Kenna made the
following statement concerning the over-taxation of
Ireland :—

The policy of the Whig Government in respect to Ireland has
been one of constant and continuous exhaustion, of exorbitant and
increasing taxation, of taxation augmented, not in proportion to
the increased requirements of the State, but augmented in the
ratio of the obvious and proven deterioration of the sources of commercial and agricultural profit in Ireland. . . . . I tell you
that to this increased taxation—unaccompanied by any fair distribution of the imperial outlay in this country—is wholly due the
fact that the battle for life is keener in Ireland, as a chronic condition, than in any other civilized country on the face of the earth.
It is in a great degree because of the heartless taxation that the
people are fleeing away.

This clear and emphatic declaration preceded the
perennial Parliamentary protests against the over-
taxation of Ireland which Sir Joseph M'Kenna was
soon to commence. He was most methodical in the
manner in which he attacked the existing financial
arrangements. He first moved for and obtained Parliamentary returns of revenue, population, resources, and
expenditure. He then subjected these to the keenest
and most subtle analysis yet made of the Financial
Relations of Great Britain and Ireland. For twenty
years he raised the question with such apparent fruit-
lessness as would have deterred a less convinced and
determined enthusiast, and during that long period
his voice seemed that of one crying in the Parliamentary

wilderness. Unchecked by defeat and undismayed by
indifference, he returned again and again to the subject.
In reality he was making headway. In those debates
in which he tried, session after session, to impress his
views on the Government of the day, he evolved canons
of international finance, the application of which to
the circumstances of Ireland made a case which neither
the public financiers nor the political economists of
England could answer, and which ultimately necessitated
exhaustive examination by the ablest experts whom it
was possible for the State to appoint. The cogency of his
reasoning, his lucid presentation of facts, and the dogged
perseverance with which he pursued his subject, places
him in the front rank of those who protested against the
over-taxation of Ireland. He was born in Dublin in
1819, educated at Trinity College, and called to the Bar
in 1848. He unsuccessfully contested New Ross in 1859
and 1863, and Tralee in 1865. He represented Youghal
from 1865 to 1868, but was defeated at the General
Election of the latter year. Re-elected for Youghal in
1874, he sat in Parliament until 1892. He gave evidence
before the Royal Commission on the 6th December,
1894. He was a director of the National Bank of
Ireland, and his connection with that great institution in
1853, when the additional taxation was imposed, gave
him exceptional opportunities of ascertaining what the
real condition of Ireland was, and his impressions are
thus graphically recorded in *The Case of Ireland Plainly
Stated* :—

The financial legislation against Ireland which has led to the
frightful disparity which now exists was initiated by Mr.
Gladstone in 1853. I remember the first step in that fatal
new departure as if it were yesterday. I am, therefore, about to
treat of a course of financial policy of which I have been a
witness since its inception. . . . Society in Ireland, which
shortly after the famine had been disturbed by the revolutionary
fever of 1848, had weathered both storms, and was passing by

F

degrees into that condition of approximate solvency which in
frugal and thrifty populations is sometimes mistaken for prosperity.

The Irish people were not, however, prosperous in 1851, 1852,
or 1853. I passed those years amongst them in the various districts and centres of their struggling agriculture and restricted
commerce. I was just as conversant with their actual state in
three of the four provinces as the doctor who issues his daily or
hourly bulletins is of his patient's condition. My bulletins in
those days were not unhopeful. That, however, is all I can say in
that direction. In 1853 I had to deal literally with thousands of
cases where the least extra strain on accruing resources would
have produced insolvency and ruin, and where nothing but the
honesty and industry of the farmers and traders could have pulled
them through. These cases were not exceptional ; they were the
majority.

I have devoted this chapter to impressing on the reader's mind
that in 1853 Ireland, still suffering from the terrible effects of the
famine of 1846-47 and the revolutionary fever of 1848, was barely
approaching convalescence, and still by no means a proper subject
for increased taxation.

On the 9th July, 1867, he formally raised the question
in Parliament by the following motion :—

That the financial policy pursued towards Ireland within the last
fourteen years has been seriously oppressive.

He said that he would treat the subject without party
spirit and without exaggeration. The remission of the
" Consolidated Annuities " in 1853 had been made the
excuse and plea for the greatest injury ever inflicted
by the Parliament of the United Kingdom on Ireland—
an injustice which was at the root of all the subsequent
discontent and disaffection—an injustice to which not
all the genius of Liberal statesmen, nor all the platitudes
of spurious political economy, could reconcile thought-
ful Irishmen. Taxation had been increased by £2,000,000
per annum, and what had followed had been natural
enough—namely, discontent, political disaffection, political complications, smouldering rebellion. The new
taxes which had been imposed, and for which no

compensating duties had been performed for the
country, had seriously impaired the condition of all
classes in Ireland. He reviewed the *per capita* taxation
in Ireland from 1841, and showed that it had been
enormously and disproportionately increased. He was
supported by General Dunne, who reiterated his conviction that the taxation of Ireland was wholly out of
proportion to her resources ; by Lord Dunkellin, who
hoped that the Government, when adjusting the financial
burdens of the next year, would consider whether there
were not grounds for the complaints made of the
injustice and inequality of taxation in Ireland ; by
Sir Frederick Heygate, who declared that no policy
could be worse than that of *equal taxation* for Ireland,
and that the subject of Irish taxation ought to be dealt
with independently of party politics ; by Mr. Synan,
who stated that the wealth of Ireland was one to nine-
teen compared with that of England, whilst taxation
was as one to nine ; by Mr. Bruen, who considered that
some small justice might be done to Ireland if taxes
were modified or reduced. Mr. Hunt, who, as Secretary for the Treasury, represented the Government in
the debate, maintained that the increase of taxation of
which complaint had been made was really evidence
of increase of material prosperity. As regards the
increasing proportion of taxation to population, he
pointed out that it was the natural consequence of a
decrease of population caused by the emigration of the
poorer people, who contributed little to the revenue.

In withdrawing his motion, Sir Joseph M'Kenna said
that the taxation of Ireland anterior to the Union had
been *one-fortieth* of the entire taxation of the United
Kingdom, that it had been *one-twelfth* in 1853, and was
then *one-ninth*.

On the 10th, 12th, 13th, and 16th March, 1868, there
was a full-dress debate on the state of Ireland, in which

all the great Parliamentary spokesmen, from Mr. Gladstone and Mr. Disraeli down, took part. Religion,
education, landlord and tenant, were all considered; but
it was reserved to Sir Joseph M'Kenna to point out
that much of what was wrong in Ireland was due to
taxation. It had a great deal to do with discontent.
Taxation was the rent paid for the use of the British
Constitution. That Constitution was a most valuable
article, but the rent the Irish people paid for the use of
it had been raised from £4,400,000 in 1853 to £6,700,000
in 1865, owing to the legislation of a Liberal Government bent on applying to Ireland what they called
equal and similar laws, the crotchet in their heads at the
time. The additional burden of £2,300,000 then imposed upon Ireland amounted to far more than the
revenue of the Protestant Church twice over. The
increased pressure of taxation had much more to do
with Irish discontent than right honourable gentlemen
opposite imagined. Mr. Lowe said in the same
debate :—

I believe it is supposed in America in Fenian circles that we tax
Ireland most unmercifully ; but the fact is rather that Ireland
taxes us.

CHAPTER XVII.

A.D. 1868 TO 1873.

MR. GLADSTONE AND MR. GOSCHEN ON ROYAL
COMMISSIONS.

MR. LYSTER O'BEIRNE, in the address issued by him to
the electors of Cashel in 1865, thus referred to taxation :

I equally reprobate the financial legislation of late years, which,
in defiance of solemn compacts, has taxed the poorest districts of
this country as heavily as the wealthiest districts of England.

On the 16th July, 1868, he asked the Chief Secretary for Ireland

Whether his attention had been directed to the inequality of taxation between Great Britain and Ireland shown by Return No. 345, printed by order of the House on 22nd June last, by which it appears that the amount of revenue for each £100 of assessed property and income tax paid by Great Britain in 1854 was £23 18s. 11½d., while that paid by Ireland was £27 15s. 11d.

By Great Britain in 1861, £21 9s. 5½d.

By Ireland in 1861, £29 2s. 11d.

By Great Britain in 1866, £17 14s.

By Ireland in 1866, £29 10s. 7½d.

And whether he proposes, during the recess, to consider this inequality of taxation with a view to its being remedied?

Mr. Sclater-Booth, in reply, said :—

The attention of Her Majesty's Government had been drawn to the return lately moved for by the hon. member, and an inquiry had been made, and was being continued, into the causes, which appeared to show, on the face of a return the hon. member referred to in his question, what was certainly not in accordance with the common impression, that the taxation of Ireland was in a higher ratio than that of England. One cause, probably, that tended to that was that the basis of Schedule A in Ireland was notoriously lower than the basis of Schedule A in England.

General Dunne and Sir Joseph M'Kenna lost their seats at the General Election of 1868. Irish Church, Irish Land, and Irish Education mainly engrossed the attention of Parliament from 1868 to 1874, and the question of Irish taxation retreated into the background, until in 1873 the Home Government Association again brought it to the front.

In a debate on the local taxation of England on 23rd February, 1869, some very important views were expressed by Mr. Goschen and Mr. Gladstone on the duties of Royal Commissions, of the bounds within which their investigations ought to be confined, and on the nature of things which did not properly come within

their sphere.   Mr. Goschen, who was President of the
Poor Law Board, said :—

He had not yet said that the grievance complained of was not a
real and serious grievance ; but he maintained that, if such a
grievance existed, there was but one tribunal which could apply a
remedy, and that was the House of Commons itself.   He did not
believe that the majority of the House would be prepared to refer a
question of policy of this kind to a Royal Commission.   Royal
Commissioners were usually appointed to inquire into intricate
and complicated questions of fact.

If, therefore, the Government did not feel it to be compatible
with their duty to refer a question of such great moment to a
Royal Commission, he trusted that no one in the House, or in the
country, would see in that determination the slightest intention to
disregard the views which had been put forward, or to ignore the
importance of the subject itself.   On the contrary, if the Government desired to get rid of a troublesome question, and to put it
aside for two or three years, no proposal could be more welcome to
them than that of hanging up the subject, as so many others had
been hung up, by agreeing to the motion for its reference to a
Royal Commission.

Mr. Gladstone said that Mr. Goschen's speech had
placed the House in possession of the views entertained by the Government, and he continued :—

The right honourable gentleman pointed out that, as in the
view of all men, and as in the view of the honourable mover of the
motion himself, the two questions of imperial and local taxation
were too inextricably mixed up together, and that to devolve upon
a Commission, under such circumstances, the examination of the
advisability of a general re-adjustment of local taxation was,
in point of fact, to place in the hands of that Commission the
question of imperial taxation, and to give the Commission that
initiative which the House would not permit its own private
members to exercise.

It can be clearly gathered from these views, first, that
the policy of determining the incidence of taxation is the
exclusive right of the House of Commons ; second, that
the proper and peculiar duty of a Royal Commission is

to inquire into intricate and complicated questions of fact ; third, that Royal Commissions are sometimes appointed to hang up troublesome questions for two or three years ; and fourth, that the re-adjustment of taxa-tion is a question which properly belongs, not to a Royal Commission, not to the private members of the House of Commons, but to the Government of the day.

CHAPTER XVIII.

A.D. 1873.

WILLIAM JOSEPH O'NEILL DAUNT AND THE IRISH HOME RULE LEAGUE.

IN 1873 the Irish Home Rule League was busy making preparations for the next General Election, and diffusing such literature as would affect the coming battle at the polls. Amongst the pamphlets issued was *A Report of the Committee appointed by the Council of the Home Government Association to examine the Financial Relations between Great Britain and Ireland and the Pressure of Taxation upon Irish Resources.* The chairman of the committee which drew it up was Mr. William Joseph O'Neill Daunt. He was born on 28th April, 1807, at Tullamore, but resided for the greater portion of his life at Kilcascan, in West Cork. His ancestors, an Anglo-Norman family long settled in Ireland, held estates in Cork. He early joined the Repeal movement, and was elected for Mallow in 1832, but unseated on petition. When the agitation for Repeal became vigorous, he was entrusted with the charge of the movement in Leinster and Scotland. After its failure he took a greater interest in the

taxation of the country than in any other public question.   He severely criticised the extension of the income tax to Ireland by Mr. Gladstone in 1853, and
assisted the agitation of 1863-64 which secured the
appointment of General Dunne's Committee. The taxation of Ireland was ever present in his mind, and in
his writings, speeches, and magazine articles, he
made frequent mention of it.   It was in some measure
due to him that the Home Rule League brought it
again prominently forward.   Mr. W. E. H. Lecky says of
him, in the Introduction to his *Diary*, that he wrote on
the financial aspects of the Union with special authority,
and that he largely contributed towards bringing the
question to the forefront.   He died on 29th June, 1894.

Mr. M'Laren, a Scotch member, had obtained a
Parliamentary return of taxation, from which it was
sought to be shown that Ireland was undertaxed.   Mr.
O'Neill Daunt, on the 15th March, 1873, wrote that he
examined the returns to find out the Irish contribution
to the Imperial Exchequer :—

I found no separate statement of the Irish revenues. The contributions of the three kingdoms are indiscriminately thrown
together, whereas, up to 1870 inclusive, the Irish payments were
separately specified. This mode of lumping British and Irish payments *en masse* facilitates mystification at our expense.

Castlereagh, when adjusting the relative taxable capacities of
Great Britain and Ireland, said that an income tax existing in both
countries would afford the best test. Pitt expressed the same
opinion. There was then no income tax in Ireland. Now we have
got one ; and tried by this test, it appears that Ireland's share of
the general wealth is not much more than a *seventeenth part*, whilst
the Imperial Government extorts from her nearly *one-ninth* of the
general revenue.   Yet our British friends cry out for more !
more !

From the office of the Home Government Association
he issued, on 17th March, the following supplementary
letter to the Home Rule address to the Irish people :—

The amount of taxation imposed on Ireland by the Imperial Government is, as we all know, exorbitant, dishonest, and grievously oppressive. Taking as a criterion of the relative taxable ability of the two islands the amount of property assessed in each to income tax, it appears that, while our national wealth is scarcely more than one-seventeenth of the general wealth of the empire, our masters wring out of us about one-ninth of the imperial taxes. Yet their greed is insatiable ; and a new valuation of Ireland is contemplated, in order to extend the basis of Irish taxation. Mr Gladstone's leading idea in governing Ireland appears to be to extract the last possible shilling from the country. He added 52 per cent. to our taxes in 1853, at a moment when we were scarcely beginning to recover from the effects of one of the most prolonged and terrible famines recorded in history.

At a public meeting held in Great Brunswick Street, Dublin, on 30th April, 1873, he moved—

That the Home Government Association appoint a committee to investigate and report on the Financial Relations of Great Britain and Ireland, and that Mr. Butt and Mr. Cornelius Denmehy be requested to act on the committee.

The motion was adopted unanimously.

At a public meeting on 3rd June, 1873, he announced that the report on the Financial Relations was in the printer's hands, and would speedily be disseminated through the kingdom. In the course of his speech he said :—

The Union, in its financial aspect, is a swindle. The English members of General Dunne's Committee seemed totally unconscious that Ireland had any separate financial claims. They ignored the fact that Great Britain at the Union owed a debt more than sixteen times larger than the Irish debt, and that Ireland had never been given one farthing of compensation for being subjected to an equality of taxation with Great Britain. Their minds were fully prepossessed with the theory of union, a union of burdens, but not a union of expenditure ; for although they were staunch friends of incorporation where money was by its means to be taken out of Ireland, yet they did not for one moment admit that incorporation gave Ireland the least right to have her own money spent within her own borders—in fact, they stoutly argued against expenditure in Ireland.

The report of the committee was finally adopted at a public meeting of the Home Government Association on 25th June, 1873, on the motion of Mr. Cornelius Dennehy, seconded by Mr. Alfred Webb.

It examined the seventh article of the Act of Union, the speeches made on it when it was under discussion, how it worked out till 1817, and then pronounced the following verdict :—

Your committee doubt if history records a more remarkable instance of audacious and gigantic fraud than this whole transaction. The kingdom of Ireland is deliberately overcharged; and when the overcharge results in national insolvency, it is availed of as a pretext for exorbitant taxation.

It then pointed out the admission made in the report of 1815, that Ireland had been subjected to a burden which experience had proved too great, and asked what was the obvious remedy in such a case pointed out by common sense and honesty. Clearly, to have fixed a contribution commensurate with Irish comparative resources. This was not done. The Act of Union pretended to protect Ireland from equality of taxation with England " until the respective circumstances of the two countries should admit of uniform taxation." If these words meant anything, they must have meant that equality of burden should not be imposed until Ireland became wealthy enough to endure it. In 1853 she was miserably poor, and her poverty was aggravated by a prolonged famine. As the condition of Irish wealth implied by the Act of Union had not occurred, Mr. Gladstone thought he could extract an argument for increased taxation from Irish poverty ; and, accordingly, he argued that as Ireland was poor, a man with £150 a year in Ireland was proportionately richer than a man with £150 a year in England, and consequently that his income was at least as fit a subject for taxation.

The special merit of this logic is, that the poorer the country the stronger the argument for taxing her.

It then examined the proceedings of General Dunne's Committee, alluded to the defection of the Irish members, the admissions made in Sir Stafford Northcote's report, and thus comments on his inept conclusions :—

> Then, as to Sir Stafford's notion that there would be hardship in transferring to Great Britain taxes to be removed from Irish shoulders, there is not the least hardship in compelling either men or nations to pay their own just debts. We have seen that the whole scope and spirit of the Act of Union, and of subsequent imperial legislation, was to subject Ireland to British burdens which she had no part in contracting, and this notwithstanding certain illusory pretexts of protection made by Lord Castlereagh and embodied in the Union statute.

It then pointed out that, in the twenty years ending 1872, Mr. Gladstone had wrung from Ireland £45,184,090 *more* taxes than had been contributed for the twenty years ending 1852 ; that the English members of General Dunne's Committee always treated Ireland as an integral part of *the empire* when burdens were concerned ; but that *the empire* only meant England when outlay was in question. It then outlined an equitable re-arrangement :—

> Each country should be separately taxed for its own pre-Union debt charge. Ireland should also bear the burden of so much of her post-Union debt as bears a true proportion to her real relative ability ; and her contribution to imperial expenses should be also proportioned to her relative ability.

Finally, its conclusions were thus summarized—

> Ireland complains that she is unjustly treated by the Imperial Parliament in respect to taxation for the following reasons :—
>
> 1.—She is entitled to a lower rate of taxation than Great Britain on account of the great disparity between the British and Irish national debts at the time of the Union, not a shilling of

which pre-Union debts has ever been paid. The British debt was then more than sixteen times larger than the Irish debt ; and solemn promises were given to Ireland that she never would be brought under the pre-Union burdens of Great Britain. But in violation of these promises, Ireland has been brought under those burdens by the equalization of her taxes with those of Great Britain ; and she never has been given an equivalent for the load thus imposed on her.

2.—Such taxes as by the Act of Union were to have been borne in common by both countries ought (in the words of Lord Castlereagh) to have been apportioned with a strict regard to the measure of Ireland's relative ability. But the Act of Union over-estimated the relative ability of Ireland, the result of which excessive estimate was necessarily to involve Ireland in enormous and disproportioned debt.

3.—Ireland affirms that this debt was fictitious, in so far as it originated in an overcharge on her comparative resources ; yet that this fictitious debt has been treated by English statesmen and by the imperial legislature as if it were morally and equitably binding upon Ireland. It has been made the pretext for extorting from Ireland amounts of revenue enormously in excess of her real relative ability ; and at this moment insatiable statesmen are engaged in new projects of augmented extortion.

4.—Ireland complains that by the financial legislation of the Imperial Parliament she is deprived of the enjoyment of her own surplus revenues, the exclusive use of which surplus the fifth clause of the seventh article of the Union professes to secure to her ; and she suffers heavy loss from the expenditure in Great Britain or elsewhere abroad of an inordinate amount of Irish revenue.

In *The Nation* of 2nd August, 1873, appears an able and exhaustive review of the *Report of the Committee of the Home Government Association on the Financial Relations of Great Britain and Ireland :—*

The total financial loss which Ireland, directly and indirectly, has sustained since the Union is now over £400,000,000 sterling. In 1855 it was estimated at £355,000,000, but this estimate did not include several important items which should have been taken into the calculation. Indeed, the direct and indirect plunder of Ireland since the Union—without estimating the loss resulting from the destruction of Irish manufactures and commerce—may be fairly set down as £500,000,000. This, certainly, is monstrous in the extreme; but the system has been so recently adjusted as to facilitate the extraction of further taxation from Ireland according to the most approved economic English theories. Acts of "amelioration" in Ireland always end in the plunder of the people.

Having referred to the imposition of taxation in 1853, the article proceeds :—

Indeed, if anything could shatter or shake the heresy of faith in Mr. Gladstone, the knowledge of his unscrupulous plunder of Ireland shown in this report should do so. It was, we believe, after imposing the income tax on Ireland that he remitted the duty on pepper, that the Irish people might have the condiment cheap to season their vegetables. It was while disendowing the Church that he managed to draw into the Imperial Exchequer large sums of money previously spent in Ireland, without the Irish people benefiting one farthing by the transaction.

The Report excited the attention of the veteran protester against over-taxation, and in a letter of 3rd September, 1873, written from Brittas, General Dunne remarked :—

I think Mr. Daunt's pamphlet on Irish taxation a capital *résumé* of the injustice done to Ireland in this important point, and I hope it will draw the attention of the Irish people with more effect than I had been able to do with my committee and the report I attempted to get adopted.

CHAPTER XIX.

A.D. 1875.

SIR JOSEPH N. M'KENNA.

ON 12th March, 1875, Sir Joseph M'Kenna again raised in the House of Commons the question of Irish taxation by the following motion :—

That the complaints which have been made that the Imperial taxation of the United Kingdom presses more severely on Ireland

than on Great Britain, and extracts a greater revenue from Ireland
in proportion to her actual means, are worthy of the earnest consideration of Her Majesty's Government, with a view to the
adoption of measures for the equitable distribution of the pressure
of taxation, so that each of the countries constituting the United
Kingdom shall contribute to the imperial revenue in proportion to
its actual means.

He said there was a certain propagation, a certain
dissemination, perhaps, he might better term it, of
plausible but illusory evidences of Irish prosperity and
progress. He called them "Dublin Castle statistics"
from their incompleteness.

They were insufficient *data*, and were consequently
calculated to mislead, and did mislead the public, and
to some extent the official mind, when they were
adduced to justify or mystify the enormous increase in
the amount of imperial taxation levied off Ireland.

Income tax returns for 1872 showed the valuation of
England as £455,000,000, and of Ireland £26,000,000.
Incomes of England exceeded those of Ireland seven-
teenfold, whilst the Irish contribution to taxation was
one-eighth.

He had, on 1st May, 1874, moved for returns, which
disclosed on their face and as a whole a system of constant and progressive financial injustice to Ireland, such
as no people who understood the subject could submit to
with patience, and such as no poor country could suffer
without injury. They showed that, side by side with
an actual reduction of ten per cent per head in Great
Britain, the taxation per head in Ireland had been
trebled. But how had all that come to pass? What
were the imposts that had squeezed all that money out
of so poor a population? To which of them did he
take exception? He objected to the excessive total
which was raised off Ireland, augmented by taxes
which were chiefly imposed at the instance of so-called

Liberal Governments; but it certainly was not their financial policy towards Ireland which had entitled them to that honourable designation. It was scarcely a figure of speech to say that since 1841—or he would take a later date to mark the epoch, and say since the famine of 1846—the British finance minister had caught the unhappy Irish people by the throat, and wrung from them sums which, were they not vouched by the returns to that House, would seem to all men as incredible as to him they appeared exorbitant and unjust.

At present the resources of Ireland—perhaps he would more accurately express it, her annual yield of profit—was disproportionately, inordinately, and, he submitted, unjustly carried off by imperial taxation. The over-taxation of Ireland represented an additional burden on Ireland heavier relatively than the annual charge on France consequent on the Prussian war indemnity, and France was seven times as populous as Ireland and thirty times as rich.

Mr. Butt formally seconded the motion.

Mr. A M. Sullivan said that the House had probably for twenty years not listened to a more important speech on the condition of Ireland than that which had been made that evening by Sir Joseph M'Kenna. He likened the figures adduced to show a slight increase in Irish progress to those relied on by baby-farmers. A child might increase a pound and a half in weight in two years, and that small increase might be the result of ill-treatment. This state of things was the fulfilment of the prophecies of Grattan and the Plunkets, who had told the Irish Parliament that incorporation with England would attract the wealth of Ireland to the greater wealth of England, and that, whereas Ireland under her own Parliament had a comparatively light taxation, she would, when joined to England, " stagger under a weight which was a feather on the shoulders of the wealthier people."

Mr. Sullivan played a considerable part in the taxation question. He was a member of the special committee of the Dublin Corporation which investigated the question in 1863, and his paper, *The Nation*, gave at all times special prominence to the many protests which were constantly being made in Ireland.

The O'Conor Don said there was nominally equality of taxation between the two countries, yet in reality there was no such equality. He quoted from Sir Stafford Northcote's Report of 1865 to show that the present system of taxation fell more heavily on Ireland than on any other part of the United Kingdom.

Sir Stafford Northcote, who was then Chancellor of the Exchequer, and Mr. Lowe, the late Chancellor of the Exchequer, replied. The latter relied again on the *Individual Taxation* argument, and said that to establish a case it must be shown that the individual Irishman must be shown to be more heavily taxed than the individual Englishman in similar circumstances. This proof could not be adduced.

The motion was negatived without a division.

CHAPTER XX.

A.D. 1874 TO 1877

MR. MITCHELL HENRY AND MR. ISAAC BUTT.

ONE of the first members returned for an Irish constituency on the Home Rule programme was Mr. Mitchell Henry. Born in Lancashire in 1826, he followed the profession of medicine, and attained to considerable eminence as surgeon to the Middlesex Hospital. His father, who was an Ulster Irishman, died in 1862, and left a very considerable fortune to his son. Mr. Mitchell Henry bought a district in Conne-mara, and built there the handsome residence of Kyle-more Castle. His kindness to and sympathy with the people, his great intellectual ability and strength of character, united to his adoption of Home Rule prin-ciples, caused him to be unanimously elected for Galway in 1871. His first parliamentary reference to the over-taxation of Ireland was on the 2nd July, 1874, on the occasion of the Home Rule debate.

He referred to the fact that the Irish contribution to the imperial revenue was increasing ; but that was not evidence of increased prosperity, but a direct cause of the nation's poverty and rapid decline. Ireland was taxed far beyond her powers, and far, indeed, beyond what she ought fairly to contribute. With all the political and social benefits Mr. Gladstone had con-ferred on Ireland, he had shown himself most inequitable in his taxation of so poor a country, and had inflicted great injury upon her. By imposing the income tax in 1853, and by equalizing the spirit duties shortly after, the revenue had been raised from about £4,500,000 to £7,000,000, a sum out of all proportion to the wealth of the country. The total wealth of Ireland was only one-seventeenth that of England, yet she contributed one-eleventh to the imperial revenue.

The defeat of Sir Joseph M'Kenna's motion of 1875 gave rise to a very vigorous agitation in Ireland in the winter of 1875-76. At a public meeting, held in the Rotunda, Dublin, on 26th October, 1875, Mr. Mitchell Henry moved—

That the financial results of the Union and the present economic condition of the country demand the serious attention of the Irish people, and afford convincing proof of the evil effects of the Union, and of the urgent necessity of restoring parliamentary institutions in Ireland.

The speech in which he supported the motion was
not alone a most masterly and comprehensive statement of the Irish case, but also most eloquent. It
was particularly telling in the force and cogency with
which it dealt with Mr. Lowe's argument of individual
taxation, and was a most effective reply. The history
of the period since the Union, the principles of the
taxation which then, as now, bore heavily on Ireland,
were all grappled with. He declared—

No wonder that English statesmen wish to substitute the
principle of the *taxation of individuals* for geographical taxation ;
but the basis of the Union was geographical taxation and relative
national ability ; and if Irishmen lose sight of this, their case is
gone.

In a passage of singular power he referred to the ruin
which had come upon Ireland :—

It was the dreadful burden of taxation imposed on Ireland by
the Union, combined with absenteeism and cruel laws, that
reduced the Irish people to the condition of the most ill-fed and
miserable people in Europe, so that when their only sheet-anchor
—the potato—failed, they had absolutely nothing to fall back
upon, but died in crowds, or, homeless and starving, were forced
to fly from the land of their birth.

At a public meeting in Dublin, held on the 2nd
November, it was unanimously resolved—

That the admirable speech delivered at the last meeting of the
League by Mr. Mitchell Henry, M.P., be printed and circulated by
the League, and that the Council be requested to take steps to
carry this into effect.

Sir Joseph M'Kenna, at the same meeting, moved :—

That the attention of the representatives of Ireland in the
Imperial Parliament is earnestly requested to the subject of the
unfair incidence of imperial taxation on the Irish people.

Dr. Ward, M.P., who seconded the motion, referred
to a recent return, which showed that the average

yearly income of an Englishman was £18; of a Scotch-
man, £13; and of an Irishman, £4. The Irishman had
to pay in taxes out of his £4 income £1 6s. 1d.;
whilst the Englishman paid in taxes only £2 9s. 1d.
out of his income of £18.

The Nation of 6th November, 1875, in an article
headed "FIFTY MILLIONS STOLEN," remarked :—

> Mr. Mitchell Henry and Sir J. M'Kenna have proved conclu-
> sively a certain inequality in imperial taxation whereby Ireland has
> been robbed of £2,500,000 a year for the past twenty years—in all
> £50,000,000 of money—over and above an equal poundage with
> Great Britain. No one has been able to answer this astounding
> charge. No one has been able to deny it.

On 9th November, 1875, at a public meeting held
under the auspices of the Home Government Association, in the Rotunda, Dublin, it was unanimously resolved :—

> That the speech of Sir Joseph N. M'Kenna on the unequal
> pressure of imperial taxation on Ireland be printed and circulated
> at the expense of the League.

The speech was subsequently printed and circulated.

Mr. Isaac Butt, Q.C., M.P., proposed the following
resolution at the same meeting :—

> That it appears expedient that steps should be taken to prepare
> a petition to Parliament against the unfair amount levied on Ire-
> land under the present arrangement of taxation, and claiming for
> this country relief from this unjust burden, either by a review of
> the relative taxation of the two countries, so as to place it upon a
> more equitable basis, or by applying the amount now collected from
> Ireland beyond her fair contribution to the relief of the local
> taxation of this country.

He stated that he had drafted a petition, but, on
account of its great importance, he preferred to have it
approved of. It was perfectly established that Ireland
contributed to the revenue of the United Kingdom an

amount far exceeding the proportion she ought to pay
according to relative ability. In that year (1875) the
imperial system of taxation was exacting from Ireland
three and a-half millions more than she ought to pay.
He then appealed to all Irishmen to unite on the over-
taxation question :—

This question of over-taxation was no Home Rule question.
It was a question on which men who were not Home Rulers might
perfectly join. It was a question for all Irishmen. It was a
grievance that might be redressed by the English Parliament, and
it was one that ought to be redressed by the English Parliament
next year if they were prepared to do it. He appealed to the Con-
servatives of Ireland—to the Conservative gentry, whose properties
were oppressed by this unjust taxation. He appealed to the Conservative Press to aid in exposing this monstrous injustice, and
in demanding redress for it. Shame would attach to the Irishman
who would keep back from exposing such an injustice, and demanding redress for it, because he might think that in so doing
he was helping the cause of Home Rule.

The earnest and determined propaganda of the Home
Rule League against over-taxation attracted the attention of *The Times*, and on the 8th November it had an
article on this " well-worn theme." It attacked Mr.
Mitchell Henry and Sir Joseph M'Kenna, and described
the latter as the Parliamentary proprietor of this special
grievance. The downright untruth of its comments
may be gathered from its statements that the proportion
of Ireland's contribution to imperial revenue

Was not fixed as an international compact at the Union,

and that Ireland was growing in wealth. It is a shallow
article, written in a narrow spirit, sneering at cheap
whisky, but nevertheless is unmistakable evidence that
the question of Irish taxation again caused anxiety in
England.

Professor Galbraith, Trinity College, Dublin, at a
public meeting on 30th November, moved :—

That this meeting views with satisfaction the printed copy, now laid on the table, of the Report of the Speech of Mitchell Henry, Member of Parliament for the County Galway, and desires to return its sincere thanks to the honourable gentleman for the zeal and great ability he has displayed in exposing the many instances of fiscal grievances which Ireland suffers from her connection with Great Britain under the terms of the legislative union.

At a Conference of the Home Rule Members of Parliament, held on 4th January, 1876, at which thirty-one were present, it was unanimously resolved that the excessive taxation of Ireland should be vigorously pressed on the attention of Parliament.

Accordingly, on 23rd May, 1876, Mr. Mitchell Henry, on the third reading of the *Customs and Inland Revenue Bill*, moved an amendment for the purpose of discussing Irish taxation :—

That, in the opinion of this House, no financial arrangements can be satisfactory which are so framed as to make no provision for relieving Ireland from a burden of taxation beyond her ability to pay as compared with Great Britain.

He said that there was no more unpopular subject in the House than Irish financial grievances, because the House believed that they were of an unsubstantial character. After long and earnest study, he had come to the conclusion that they were of a substantial and practical nature. He affirmed that within the last twenty-three years the taxation of Ireland had been doubled, whilst the population had declined by 2,500,000 persons. During the past five years £42,000,000 had been raised in taxes ; and of the annual levy of £8,500,000, nearly £6,500,000 were raised in customs and excise duties, and were paid by the poorer classes of people. Having alluded to Mr. Lowe's individual taxation argument, he continued :—

The case of Ireland is that by this heavy taxation you have removed, and do remove, such an immense proportion of the

income of the country, that not only have the people been obliged
to fly to happier climes to gain a livelihood, but there is nothing
left to develop the resources of the country.   The country is borne
down by the excessive character of the taxation, and the abject
and miserable poverty, the result in part of it, is one of the chief
causes of discontent in Ireland.

He pointed out that the burden of taxation was
infinitely and shamefully heavier in Ireland than in
England.   He compared the total annual incomes of
England and Ireland, and showed that taxation in
England amounted only to 1s. 8d. in the pound, whilst
in Ireland it amounted to 3s. 4d. in the pound.   He
challenged contradiction on this, and was prepared
to refer it to arbitration.   He showed the severity of
local taxation in Ireland, and that exemptions of
assessed taxes were a mere bagatelle compared with
the excessive exactions.   He pointed out the decay
which had taken place in almost every industry in
Ireland, and that emigration was due to excessive
taxation.   He concluded by appealing to the Irish
members on both sides of the House to support his
amendment.

The O'Conor Don seconded the amendment, and said
that the belief sedulously fostered in the press that
Ireland was lightly taxed was the greatest fallacy that
ever existed.   Indirect taxation bore severely on the
Irish community, which, as a whole, was poorer and less
able to bear the burden than the English people.

The Irish members who joined in the debate were
Sir Joseph M'Kenna, Dr. Ward, and Mr. Isaac Butt,
who said:—

When they had a community, they could not take away money
from the community without injuring it.   From the time of the
Union down to the present day, the finance of Ireland had always
been dealt with as something belonging to a separate community,
and when remissions were made in favour of any class in Ireland,
they always heard of the boons granted to that country.

Sir Stafford Northcote, who was Chancellor of the Exchequer, replied for the Government, and took up a hostile attitude.

The amendment was withdrawn by leave.

In the course of a long article on the debate, *The Nation* of 3rd June wrote :—

> We need scarcely ask our readers to give an attentive perusal to the important speech of Mr. Mitchell Henry on Irish taxation. The proofs and arguments there adduced to show that Ireland is overweighed in this respect are simply unanswerable. No amount of quibbling and glozing on the part of English Chancellors of the Exchequer, past or present, can disprove the hard facts brought forward by the Member for Galway.

The Times of 30th May referred to Sir Stafford Northcote's *colourless summary* of a report adopted by General Dunne's Committee in 1865, and thus proceeds :—

> This was eleven years ago, and since that time the subject has been raised, we know not how many times, by Irish members emulous of distinction. They turn to it again and again, now one and now another leading the attack, and always in face of them is this stronghold of Mr. Lowe's position, that they can no more turn than we can turn the conclusions of the fourth proposition of the first book of Euclid. Yet it does not, as far as we can discover, disconcert them in the least.

The usual abuse about whisky was reiterated, and Sir Stafford Northcote was complimented on having advanced from his statement of 1865, that—

> With equal taxation the tax will press more heavily upon the poorer than upon the richer country

to the adoption of the severer doctrine of Mr. Lowe of individual taxation.

The subject was again raised in the House of Commons by Mr. Mitchell Henry, in a set motion, on 5th June, 1877 :—

(1) That the burden of imperial taxation imposed on Ireland is excessive and out of proportion to her financial ability to bear it as compared to England.

(2) That this inequality is a violation of the promises made at the Union, and occasions a loss of capital which, accompanied by the annual absentee drain, is the main cause of the small material progress of the country.

(3) That to tax a poor country on the same scale as a rich one is in itself unjust and opposed to sound economic principles; whilst the fact that the excessive taxation raised in Ireland is in great measure expended out of Ireland forms an aggravation of the injustice, and makes permanent improvement hopeless until the present mode of dealing with Irish revenues is altered.

In the speech in which he introduced it, he said that the more he studied it the more he saw the iniquity of the present arrangement. He believed that the misery that occurred in Ireland—and the miseries that occurred in England owing to her connection with Ireland—had arisen in a large measure from the financial relations of the two countries. He then made an able, exhaustive review of Irish fiscal history, and asked, How had Ireland been treated of late? The answer was: In the last twenty-five years the taxation of Ireland had been doubled. She then paid £8,500,000 to the finances of England, against £4,000,000 paid twenty-five years previously. During twenty-five years her population diminished one-half, which meant that Ireland was paying four times as much as she paid twenty-eight years previously. If the Irish people were foolish enough to give up the question of geographical taxation, their case was gone. Ireland should be taxed in proportion to her financial ability as compared with England. It was not a question of individual taxation. It was the question of the taxation of a nation. Ireland was treated as a man treated a field when he took a crop of grass off it every year and never bought any manure to put on the ground. The man expected the field to go on yielding him crops, but in time it became barren.

Mr. Butt said, if they selected any tax which fell heavier on the people of Ireland than on the people of England, they undoubtedly placed a greater burden on the one country than on the other.

Mr. Mitchell Henry, in closing the debate, said that the question was one full of complications, and a vast amount of labour was required to get behind it ; but it would recur and become better understood every year by the Irish people, and he believed they would soon learn the various forms the question assumed and make it worth while for the Chancellor of the Exchequer to meet their complaints.

The motion on this occasion was pressed to a division, and there voted for 34, and against 152. The minority included J. G. Biggar, I. Butt, E. W. Grey, Mitchell Henry, Sir Joseph M'Kenna, Charles S. Parnell, O'Connor Power, W. A. Redmond, and A. M. Sullivan. The tellers for the minority were Captain Nolan and Richard Power.

———————

CHAPTER XXI.

A.D. 1882.

SIR J. M'KENNA MOVES FOR A SELECT COMMITTEE ON IRISH TAXATION. THE HOUSE COUNTED OUT.

ON 18th April, 1882, Sir Joseph M'Kenna asked for the appointment of a select committee

To inquire and report whether, since the year 1851, the new and additional duties which have been levied off Ireland have not increased the pressure of imperial taxation on the population of that portion of the United Kingdom to such an extent that, having regard to the total property and income of the inhabitants of each island respectively, the imperial taxation of Ireland is now doubly

heavier than that of Great Britain ; whether the entire imperial
taxation of Great Britain does not barely exceed the produce of an
income tax of 2s. 6d. in the pound, and whether that of Ireland
does not exceed what would be produced by an income tax of
5s. 3d.

He said there was no finding of the committee of
1865 which anticipated, answered, or decided in any
way upon the issue raised by the present motion, which
was one for the appointment of a committee to inquire
into a state of facts without parallel in modern history,
and into a course of legislation for the last twenty-nine
years which had led to results without precedent in this
or in any other country of the world.   Calling things
by hard names and bad names was not his habit, for
that was neither proof nor argument.   It was impossible to find words in which to describe the financial
policy pursued towards Ireland since 1853 unless one
had recourse to very strong terms.   His chief difficulty
was, not to be moderate in referring to the injustice
which had been done, but to find words to describe
the ignorance of honourable members in former Parlia-
ments and in this on the subject.   Even this lack of
information was scarcely so remarkable as the self-com-
placency with which those honourable members seemed
to contemplate the conduct of Great Britain and this
Parliament towards Ireland in modern times ; for it was
not infrequent to hear the fiscal legislation of the United
Kingdom referred to as if Ireland were in that respect
a favoured and cherished sister.   There never was a
greater delusion.   There was no country in Europe in
which so large a proportion of the total income of a man
was levied by the State taxman as in Ireland.   To
assume that identity of imposts in all cases meant
equality of taxation was a monstrous delusion.   The
articles selected for taxation should be equally in
demand, equally used, and equally consumed in both

countries, otherwise identity of imposts meant the very
opposite to equality of taxation. A moderate tax on
cheese would fall heavily on the bulk of the English
people, and would scarcely affect the Irish in the least.
Raising the taxation of Ireland in 1853 was the modern
method of sowing dragons' teeth, with a parallel result
to the ancient precedent. From 1853 Dublin Castle
represented Ireland as making great strides towards
material prosperity, whilst the country was really
struggling in vain against the wasting process. The
logical corollary to Mr. Lowe's argument of *individual
taxation* was that France and Tunis were two geographical expressions, and that a heavy tax on dates
and a light tax on grapes would be fair between the
French and Tunisians. Aesop's fable of *The Fox and
the Stork* had long since put boyhood and manhood on
their guard against such shallow sophistry. He went
into elaborate figures to justify his views.

Two efforts were made to count the House out, the
second of which was successful before he had concluded.
Discussion was stopped for the time being ; but some
more powerful exorcism than a *count out* was necessary
to lay the spirit of the gigantic crime perpetrated on
Ireland.

When Sir Joseph M'Kenna was refused a hearing by
the House of Commons, he addressed the English
people in a pamphlet, published in 1883 in London :
Imperial Taxation : The Case of Ireland Plainly Stated.
Its forty-six pages bristle with facts. The transparent
clearness of its homely style merits its title. It is rich
in economic aphorisms. Its brevity is commendable,
its reasoning irresistible, its deductions convincing, and
its conclusions unanswerable. It proceeds from cause
to effect with logical sequence, and enunciates canons
of international taxation with striking clearness and
originality. Viewed in the light of the Report of the

Royal Commission, it is a marvel of prophecy. The following extracts, all of which will be found useful in the present controversy, are made from it :—

Political oppression in modern times is mostly financial.

The true principle of taxation is to raise the minimum amount necessary for the needs of the State with the most equitable distribution of its incidence.

The justice or injustice of imposing a particular tax does not altogether depend on the nature of the impost itself, for a particular tax may be fair enough in the abstract, yet unjust in its application. For instance, there may be eight subjects for taxation, each equally proper in the abstract to sustain an impost ; but if from five of these the State has already gathered the full amount which the community ought to pay on all, the three subjects which had hitherto escaped taxation should remain untaxed until the burden could be equitably distributed over the entire.

The evils inflicted on Ireland, and the benefits which accrued to England owing to the financial system of 1853.

Thus the policy of 1853, which impoverished Ireland, has marched together with the reduction of English taxes and repayment of the national debt, *pari passu*, in grand procession for thirty years.

The Chancellor of the Exchequer of an empire ought to be able to establish a system of identical imposts, with safeguards for the readjustment of any unequal incidence.

The science of political federation, and of the distribution of taxation and revenue in empires, has advanced sufficiently to enable any accomplished Chancellor or statesman to propound a perfectly equitable scheme for the maintenance of identical imposts throughout an empire made up of many states, with populations of various habits of living, containing provisions to redress any unequal incidence of the levies as they first affect the respective peoples or divisions of which the empire is composed.

The comparative wealth and poverty of states constituting an empire must be taken into account when adjusting taxation between them.

Before pronouncing the taxation of any country fair or unfair, if the country be one of several constituting an empire or confederation, the taxation must be viewed in relation to the comparative wealth or poverty of the inhabitants of the respective countries which constitute the empire or confederation. The actual sum contributed, without other data, is no guide whatever.

The Irish case for redress of over-taxation is unanswerable.

The injustice towards Ireland in the matter of imperial taxation is so great, that nothing but the shallowest and silliest substitutes for argument are ever adduced, or are adducible, in defence of the present system.

CHAPTER XXII.

A.D. 1886.

SIR JOSEPH M'KENNA MOVES FOR RETURNS.

MR. GOSCHEN SUGGESTS A COMMITTEE OF INQUIRY.

THE disastrous termination of his motion for a select committee in 1882 neither silenced nor deterred Sir Joseph M'Kenna, and again, on 23rd February, 1886, he returned to the subject with the same irrepressible ardour and determination. At different intervals during the previous twenty years he had vainly tried to arrest the attention of the House of Commons ; but at length he was to receive a patient and sympathetic hearing. He moved for a

Return of the gross imperial revenue of Ireland derived from taxation and of the population of Ireland for the years 1851, 1861, 1871, and 1881, and a like return for Great Britain for the same years, being in both cases a continuation, in like form, of Parliamentary Paper No. 407 of Session 1874.

In moving for the return, he alluded to the " count out," by means of which the Government officials thought fit to put an end to the discussion in 1882. There was no danger of that to-night ; but if English and Scotch members attended to him, they would understand many things connected with Ireland which, at first sight, did not appear to be connected with imperial taxation. He did not accuse any party of intentional injustice to Ireland in the matter of imperial taxation. He was content with showing how the taxation of Ireland increased in the face of a waning population, whilst the taxation of Great Britain had been so regulated and the revenue husbanded that the pressure of taxation was continuously lightened, so that, whilst it increased in amount, its incidence on each head of the population was constantly growing lighter. He quoted Adam Smith's canons of taxation, and asserted that they had been grievously violated in the case of Ireland. He mentioned that the taxation per head in Ireland in 1841 was 9s. 6½d. (which was very severe), and in 1871 it was £1 6s. 1d.

Adam Smith's rule that taxation should be levied on the subjects of a state in proportion to the incomes they enjoyed under its protection applied in strongest force to empires made up of several nationalities, where the possessions of an entire people could be measured with approximate accuracy. He was told that the taxation per head of the people of Great Britain greatly exceeded the taxation per head of the people of Ireland. Yes, but the taxation per head of the people of Ireland was five times that per head of the people of India ; but that did not prove that the people of India were not more heavily taxed than the people of Ireland. Taxation ought to be estimated and levied according to wealth. He adduced the comparison per head of population simply to show that there was progressive

alleviation in the case of Great Britain, and an extraordinary progressive increase of burden in Ireland. His
legitimate arguments on the relative powers of Great
Britain and Ireland to sustain taxation had been met
with every form of evasion.   One right honourable
gentleman, a Chancellor of the Exchequer, who then
adorned the Upper House, had the temerity to say that
Ireland was not taxed at all, but that the individuals
who happened to reside in Ireland were taxed ; that the
taxation was just, as the same tariff was applied in
Ireland and Great Britain ; and he thus disposed of all
grievance, ignoring that unless the habits of the people
of Great Britain and Ireland were identical, and their
wealth relatively equal, identity of impost was no
guarantee of equality of taxation.   Another right
honourable gentleman, who had been translated to the
same convenient haven, admitted the general facts, and
that a case of disparity was made out, but raised the
phantom of an argument that greater disparity might
be shown between districts in England.   Not the
slightest attempt was made to show why the taxation
of Ireland should have been increased by £3,000,000 a
year contemporaneously with a decrease of 3,000,000 of
the inhabitants of the unfortunate country.   In no part
of the world did so monstrous a system of fiscal injustice
prevail as that of the United Kingdom towards Ireland.
He attributed no malign designs to anyone, and it was
for the curious to determine whether this was the work
of the permanent officials or of the gentlemen who held
Her Majesty's seals.   The whole imperial taxation of
England could be commuted by an income tax of 2s. 6d.
in the pound.   The whole imperial taxation of Ireland
could not be commuted at less than an income tax of
5s. 3d. in the pound.   He had heard *ad nauseam* that
there was nothing abnormal in the taxation of Ireland,
that she was a favoured nation, treated with sisterly self-

sacrificing affection by Great Britain ; yet the highest
statistical authority in the service of the Government
recently confessed that Ireland ought not to fairly contribute more than half her present contribution.   He
then dealt with the case suggested in mitigation, namely,
that of expenditure :—

As a matter of account between the imperial exchequer and
Ireland, the locality in which the charge for imperial objects was
expended had nothing to do with the distribution of the burden of
the charge.   He freely admitted that the local trade of the district
in which imperial funds were expended benefited somewhat by
the expenditure ; but that was not the point, and had no earthly
connection with the distribution of the charge amongst the taxpayers of Great Britain and Ireland.

Sir Thomas Esmonde seconded the motion.   Ireland
was overtaxed, having regard to the amount of the Irish
national debt at the time of the Union, and having
regard to the poverty of the people compared with the
people of England.   He made a complete and careful
analysis of the Irish and English debts before and after
the Union to show the unfair treatment in that respect.
The second objection to the present taxation was the
absence of manufactures and commercial enterprise
from Ireland.

Mr. Goschen expressed his sense of the extreme importance of the question raised by Sir Joseph M'Kenna.
He regretted that the matter had not been dealt with
at an earlier stage.   If there was an Irish case, everyone
must be most anxious to examine it to the very bottom,
and those who were anxious to maintain the legislative
Union felt all the more bound to see that no financial
injustice was done to a country which was in a minority
in the House.   Every motion which came from the Irish
quarter substantiating even a *prima facie* case of financial injustice ought to be probed to the bottom.   The
fact that a distinguished statistician had stated that

Ireland was paying too much towards imperial taxation added additional importance to the motion. He then stated that a return would not be sufficient to show whether Ireland was paying too much or too little, and then remarked :—

What will some time or other be necessary, if it is not done on the present occasion, is that the principles (of *taxable capacity*) should be grappled with by a committee or otherwise, and that then, applying those principles, we should see whether or not we could come to some agreement. I am sure the bulk of the population of both countries would wish to come to a fair agreement upon this matter. I have thought myself of moving to substitute a committee on this occasion for a return ; but I have reason to believe that that, in the present position of Irish affairs, would not be a very convenient arrangement, and I further think it will be wise, and may advance the matter, if the return should be procured without any delay. But if nothing should come of the presentation of the return, I trust at some future period that this question may be renewed, and that we may endeavour by some such means as may be in our power to probe this very important question to the very bottom to see if a grievance exists, and, if a grievance really exists, to set to work to remedy it in a spirit of justice and equity to all parts of the United Kingdom.

Mr. John Dillon, Mr. J. F. X. O'Brien, and Colonel Nolan spoke from the Irish benches.

Mr. Gladstone (First Lord of the Treasury) spoke of the excellent spirit which pervaded the debate. Committees were appointed to examine this question and of "bolting it to the bran." The committee of 1863-64 (*sic*) was appointed to determine whether Ireland paid excessively or not in proportion to her means. Yet that committee came to no conclusion and made no report upon that portion of the subject. The committee gave great attention and labour to the general investigation, yet gave the go-by to that question, for the simple reason that it could not arrive at any amount of unanimity, even by a majority. He considered that

income tax was not a sufficient test of relative ability,
but that the average of legacy and succession duties for
a number of years was the fairest test which could be
obtained. He admitted that the proportion of two to
fifteen fixed at the time of the Union was too high.
He concluded :—

I beg members to remember that this is a subject that does not
bear being handled by demonstrative evidence. Debate it as long
as you will, appoint as many committees as you will, it will still be
in the main a matter of argument. The best security and guarantee
we can have for arriving with tolerable facility at some tolerably
fair conclusion is that all gentlemen should endeavour to approach
the question in a thoroughly considerate spirit, and with an abate-
ment of all extreme opinions. If they do that, I believe the matter
is perfectly capable of a practical solution ; and it is because I think
the temper that has been shown to-night affords considerable promise of progress in that direction, should the necessity arise, that
I congratulate the honourable gentleman and the House upon the
spirit with which the debate has been conducted.

An explanation of the very remarkable change in the
demeanour of both English parties on the question of
Irish taxation must be sought in the political circumstances of the time. Irish complaints, so often made in
the past, had almost invariably been met with callous
indifference. Nevertheless, the great change of attitude,
irrespective of the motives which prompted it, was a
hopeful augury for the future of the Irish case.

CHAPTER XXIII.

A.D. 1886.

" THE TIMES," LORD MONTEAGLE, AND SIR ROBERT GIFFEN.

THE remarkable change in English public opinion was manifested more clearly in the columns of *The Times* than even in the discussion in the House of Commons. The infallibility of past years of that journal was laid aside, and instead it adopted a mild agnosticism towards such difficult problems as incidence of taxation and the tests by which the capacity of contribution was to be measured, on which it was wont to dogmatize so incontrovertibly. On the 24th February, 1886, it expressed the following views :—

We cordially agree with Mr. Goschen that those who are most strongly in favour of maintaining the legislative Union ought to be the readiest to support a demand for inquiry by the Imperial Parliament into every case of alleged grievance that can be supported by any show of reason and by anything approaching to trustworthy evidence. . . . A committee to inquire into the subject—though the Prime Minister reminded the House that previous inquiries, of which there have been many, resulted in no decisive conclusions—would appear to be desirable. The actual incidence of taxation has to be determined, as well as the tests by which the capacity of contribution is to be measured, and at present there is the widest diversity of opinion on both points.

*   *   *   *

We are inclined to think, therefore, that Sir John Lubbock is right in questioning whether an inquiry would show any kind of unfairness to Ireland in respect of her fiscal burdens as compared with the rest of the United Kingdom. But that is no reason why Mr. Goschen's suggestion of a select committee, which even Mr. Dillon recognised as conceived in a kindly spirit, should not be adopted.

In *The Times* of 27th February, Lord Monteagle expressed satisfaction at the spirit of conciliation displayed in the recent debate, and hoped it would continue to prevail. He then discussed the "relative ability" of the two countries—a question on which the widest diversity of opinion prevailed :—

(*a*) The exports and imports of Ireland for the year 1882 amounted to eleven millions, and those of the United Kingdom to 720 millions, giving a proportion of 1 : 65.

(*b*) The customs and excise of Ireland for the same year amounted (as far as I can ascertain) to six millions, and those of the United Kingdom to forty-six millions, giving a proportion of 2 : 15.

(*c*) Taking the proportion of population, which is 1 : 7, the three together give a proportion of 1 : 21, which is singularly close to the income tax test, viz., 1 : 20.

But public attention was still more earnestly focussed on the taxation of Ireland by the remarkable contribution to the March number of *The Nineteenth Century*, 1886, by Sir Robert Giffen. He was chief of the Statistical Department of the Board of Trade, and his reputation was second to none in England as a sound thinker and writer on economics and finance. Not the least noticeable feature of his opinions was his marked tendency to adopt optimistic views on the seriously debated questions of his time which related to the material well-being of England. His pictures of economic England and economic Ireland contrast as sharply as Dante's visions of the *Paradiso* and *Inferno*. Painting darkness and decay was a task as unusual to him as it was uncongenial, and was done in the case of Ireland because no other picture was possible. His official position, and the admitted authority of his opinions, ensured a wide discussion for the article. It estimated the economic value of Ireland to Great Britain mainly from the English standpoint. It noticed the relative and absolute increase of population in England, and the relative and absolute decrease in Ireland. It showed that the residuum of people remaining in Ireland was not equal in industrial character and resources to an equal number of the people of Great Britain. The taxable income of Ireland was so low, and its resources so slender, that, as a partner of a rich state like Great Britain, Ireland was insignificant, and hardly counted one way or the other. He summed up his conclusions on Irish decline in the following graphic paragraph :—

To put the matter shortly and in the roundest figures—there can, of course, be no exact figures of income and capital—Ireland, in population, has sunk from one-third to less than one-seventh in gross income, from two-seventeenths to less than one-seventeenth ; in capital, from a proportion that was material to about one-twenty-fourth only ; in taxable resources, from a proportion that was also material, being, perhaps, about one-tenth, to a proportion that is almost inappreciable—the proportion of only one to fifty. In resources Ireland has, no doubt, increased absolutely. The Irish people are much better off individually, partly because there are fewer people than there were fifty years ago, but with much the same resources ; but as a community in relation to Great Britain there is an immense decline.

When he came to write on Irish taxation, he merely re-echoed the Irish complaints of thirty years, though, admittedly, the discovery by him was new, and the result of his own investigations—

I desire likewise to call attention to the fact, which has come out incidentally, that Ireland is overtaxed in comparison with Great Britain. It contributes twice its proper share, if not more, to the Imperial Exchequer. The taxation in one view is not reprehensible ; it is levied in the shape of indirect taxes, mainly on spirits and tobacco. The Irish masses could untax themselves by the simple expedient of consuming less spirits and tobacco. This is the easy view which has often been acted upon when the subject has come up in the Imperial Parliament. Long ago, in 1864, when there was a committee on Irish taxation, Mr. Lowe embarrassed an able witness, Mr. E. Senior, a poor law inspector in Ireland, and well acquainted with Irish poverty, by putting this very point. But it is not the right view. How much of the expenditure of the Irish people on spirits and tobacco is really wasteful is not certainly known. People who have so little taxable income have, at any rate, a claim to have the money taken from them by the Government applied for their special benefit. At present nearly the whole taxable income of the Irish people is, in fact, absorbed by the State. The taxable income being about £15,000,000 only, the Imperial Government, as we have seen, takes nearly £7,000,000, and local taxes are over £3,000,000 more, or about £10,000,000 in all. So large a proportion of taxation to taxable income would be a serious fact for any country, and there can be little accumulation in Ireland under such conditions.

CHAPTER XXIV.

A.D. 1886-87.

MR. C. S. PARNELL AND SIR J. N. M'KENNA.

MR. BOYLE O'REILLY, of *The Boston Pilot*, made inquiries of Sir Joseph M'Kenna early in 1886 about the financial provisions of the Home Rule Bill. The interrogatories were thus summarized by Sir Joseph M'Kenna:—

" Do these (financial) clauses provide for any sufficient alteration in the incidence of taxation to remedy the evils which you demonstrated in your pamphlet on *Imperial Taxation* (Rivingtons, 1883) which you were good enough to send me ? I ask because they do not appear to me to do so."

These questions were submitted to Mr. Parnell, and he re-read Sir Joseph M'Kenna's pamphlet of 1883. The interview which took place between Mr. Parnell and Sir Joseph M'Kenna is thus recorded by Sir

Joseph in *The Irish Daily Independent* of 6th August, 1892 :—

" He next asked me if, on the hypothesis that he considered that my views were right, I thought he would be justified in maintaining silence about them to Mr. Gladstone. I answered that, in my opinion, it would be right for him to say to Mr. Gladstone that he (Mr. Parnell) was aware that certain members of the party, who had promised to support the Bill on the second reading, had told him that they would go for amendments in committee, without which they would regard the financial clauses as oppressive. Mr. Gladstone, I presumed, would say to him, and I believe subsequently did, that all reasonable amendments would have fair consideration. I advised that in such case the subject should not be followed up until the second reading had passed.

" Mr. Parnell then asked me if I could give him the texts of the amendments to consider. I offered an objection to doing so, which Mr. Parnell accepted. I told him that it would only embarrass him to have them so as to have to admit to Mr. Gladstone that they had been already formulated. Mr. Parnell then said to me, ' I trust implicitly to your knowledge of the subject, and that you will be able to give me in good time the text of all amendments you think vital, and we shall confer as to who had best move each.' I answered Mr. Parnell *on this head* to the exact effect of what I now indite."

" ' The amendments which I will formulate shall be very few, and such as will commend themselves, *by the equities on the face of them*, to every dispassionate mind. Some of the most objectionable clauses will be adequately met by allowing the words of the Bill to stand, and interpolating the words *save as hereinafter*. My amendments need not be verbose ; they would be mostly, if not wholly, in the nature of *provisoes.* I would

aim at getting the Irish Secretary and Irish Attorney-
General (with Mr. Gladstone's approval) to assent to
most of them without controversy in committee, or to
propose them. I would allow Mr. Gladstone a very free
hand apparently to pile up, as he has done in prospect,
burdens on Ireland's future revenue; but I would *unload*
them all again by the *proviso that the total contribution
of Ireland to imperial revenue should not exceed the proportion of the revenue relatively to the income tax exacted from
England and Wales* by the Imperial Parliament.'"

"Mr. Parnell then asked, 'Can this be done practically?' I answered, 'Yes; it only involves another
ledger in the Treasury and a corresponding one in
Dublin. Mr. Robert Giffen will be easily able to
show Mr. Gladstone, *if there be the will, what the way
is.* We shall only ask what is fair, and I promise
you there shall be no equitable flaw in any one of
our provisoes.'"

"When we had got so far in our conversation, Mr.
Parnell had nearly read over—as I believe for the
second time—my pamphlet of 1883. He then asked
in a very kind fashion, 'Would it be too much,
M'Kenna, to ask you to write another pamphlet on
nearly the same lines, but, if possible, not driving so
hard as this one does at Gladstone, but showing
what we could do for ourselves *on the Land Question* if
our means had not been mopped up by the imperial
tax-gatherer since the Union?'"

"I answered, 'If you wish it, I shall do so certainly;
but I shall require some fresh returns to justify me in
issuing a fresh pamphlet. I will move at once for the
requisite papers, and perhaps Mr. Gladstone will let me
have them. The pamphlet Mr. Boyle O'Reilly writes
upon is, I believe, *quite out of print*, and, except a few
copies which I early retained for myself or for our own
party, they are not to be had for love or money.'"

" Shortly after this conversation, whilst Mr. Gladstone was still in power in 1886, I moved for the requisite returns, which Mr. H. Fowler, then Secretary of the Treasury, with Mr. Gladstone's concurrence, at once assented to grant. I subsequently prepared, *agreeably with my promise to Mr. Parnell*, a fresh *résumé* of the Irish financial case as against Great Britain, starting from the passing of the Union at the end of A.D. 1800, and brought down to 1880. This is the pamphlet published by and at Ridgway's, Piccadilly (1887), where it is still to be had. Mr. Gladstone's Cabinet had retired from office in 1886, not on the rejection of the Home Rule Bill, but as the result of the General Election which followed its rejection in that year.

" Mr. Parnell, to whom I sent proofs of the pamphlet of 1887 before I would authorize its issue, commenced to read them in my presence. He observed soon that he thought I had shown too little tenderness for Mr. Gladstone in paragraphs 60, 61, 62, and 63, considering his position towards us since 1886. I offered to strike the paragraphs out ; but I excused their appearance in the proof, because the English Liberals, I said, particularly the Radical section of them, were steeped in ignorance and prejudice, and continually prated when some morsel of relief was proposed for Ireland, as if to propose such a thing were a fraud on the English tax-payer ; and I thought it needful that some one should, in forcible language, say something *per contra*, although it may not be agreeable for some of them to read that this Irish cause of ours is *not one of ancient history*, but mainly one of the present era. When I had said this, Mr. Parnell, who had previously put his pencil through the four paragraphs, bracketed them anew, and wrote 'stet' in the margin.

" When Mr. Parnell came to paragraph 90 (of the 100 paragraphs of which the pamphlet of 1887 is made up),

he said, ' I was about saying to you you had forgotten
to point out how the Land Question was only part of
the financial one, but I see that you forget nothing.'
He then read the remaining ten paragraphs slowly to
himself without saying a word, and then remarked,
' Now I know why you desired to retain the three or
four paragraphs I at first objected to. You were right;
it is a great satisfaction to me that you re-wrote the
case in plain English, and that it is on record. I am
sincerely obliged to you.'

" This is all I have now to say; but every line which I
have written in this letter is part of the case which
Ireland has to consider if Mr. Gladstone assumes power,
Mr. Gladstone is, doubtless, a wiser man than when, an
admirer of the Union, in 1853, he made such wonderful
concessions to the British taxpayer, and so far as Ireland
was concerned simply made *a grab in the dark*. The
only defence of Mr. Gladstone's conduct in 1853 is that
he was, in fact, then *in the dark;* he did not know what a
horrid business the Union was, and so he made it worse
than ever by levying fresh and oppressive taxation off
Ireland under its powers.

"Home Rule or no Home Rule, what has to be done
is to appropriate to Irish purposes *solely* the three millions
sterling a year, or whatever it may be, more or less, which
the English Government now raises from Ireland in
excess of the proportion which she ought to bear as
measured by the yield of the income tax in England,
Scotland, and Ireland."

In the debate on the Home Rule Bill on 8th April,
1886, Mr. Parnell made the following statement on the
relative ability of Ireland :—

I have every conviction—I do not want to go into the question
to-night, but after carefully reading the article by Mr. Giffen,
which has attracted so much attention, and a long communication
which appears in *The Times* of this morning from a gentleman who

evidently knows what he is writing about. I am convinced that it is clear that one-twentieth is a far better standard of the relative share of the two countries than that most unfortunate standard of one-fifteenth which the right hon. gentleman has adopted. We could show several standards much more favourable to us, based upon the various commodities consumed in Ireland, and which will show that Ireland is a very much poorer country in comparison with England than is expressed by the proportion which the right hon. gentleman has selected. I have every confidence that when the time comes when this Bill is in committee, and when we put forward our case, the conscience not only of the House of Commons, but of the right hon. gentleman the Chancellor of the Exchequer, will be touched in regard to this matter, and that the Prime Minister will see that his zeal for making a good bargain for his own country in imperial questions has misled him into doing an unintentional injustice to Ireland in regard to this question of the contribution towards the imperial expenditure.

Sir Joseph M'Kenna wrote the pamphlet as requested by Mr. Parnell, and it was published in the following year. The Parliamentary returns which he had moved for in February had been issued, and enabled him to bring his case up to date. The pamphlet of 1883 differs very much from that of 1887. The former was confined to an examination of the over-taxation from 1853 ; the latter reviews the whole period since the Union. The taxation raised in Ireland from 1800 to 1850 was compared with the taxation raised from 1856 to 1881. In other words, the taxation of the first fifty years of the Union was compared with the last twenty-five :—

The fiscal results of the first half-century, so far as Ireland was concerned, *and is*, are before us : the sum of £216,190,567 comprises not only all the legitimate and reasonable taxation of the half-century, but also—so far as they involve money payments within the fifty years—all the corruptions and exactions made to fall on Ireland in connection with the business of the Union. Let me not minimize the total. I have ample reason to charge it as excessive, and if I refrain now from doing so, it is because I have to compare the total exactions of the first fifty years of the Union with a much worse period which ensued, in respect of which the framers of the Union are in no sense responsible, save that, when they were all in their graves, Mr. Gladstone proposed and carried through the Imperial Parliament such measures of unjust financial exaction as would have been impossible in a native Parliament.

I proceed now to compare the first fifty years of Union taxation with the twenty-five latest years included in the returns of 17th September, 1886. If nothing abnormal had occurred—if the taxation of a famine-stricken and continuously dwindling population had only kept pace with the average taxation from the Union up to 1851—the taxation for the twenty-five years up to March, 1881, would have amounted to £108,095,283, and no more ; but instead of that sum the imperial taxation of Ireland for the twenty-five years amounted to £168,741,237.

I wonder whether people generally, without something in the nature of a rebellion to stimulate their cogitative faculties, can realize what it is to the inhabitants of a poor country to be shorn in this fashion of £60,645,945 sterling in twenty-five years, *in excess of a taxation which was itself excessive,* for it was on a scale that sufficed to appease the utmost avidity or rapacity which, with any show of reason, can be charged against the British Parliament and Government for the first fifty years of the Union.

The following analysis of the imperial taxation of the United Kingdom was the clearest and subtlest yet made, and most graphically represented the excessive taxation of Ireland :—

I commend to the careful consideration of English statesmen the following analysis, constructed from the latest dissected returns we have of the actual and relative gross amounts of revenue derived from taxation of the United Kingdom and of the three realms respectively.

The figures analysed are founded on those given in Parliamentary Return 108, of April 13th, 1886, and apply to the financial year 1884-85. The respective totals are as follows :—

England and Wales,	*total taxation,*	...	£57,327,686
Scotland,	do. do.	...	8,825,941
Ireland,	do. do.	...	7,755,001
	Total,	...	£73,908,628

An income tax for all practical purposes identical, and fairly enough designed to be of identical relative incidence, applies to all three countries.

The yields from income tax contained in the above and from *all
other imperial* taxes for each of these realms are as follows :—

	Income Tax.	All Other Imperial Taxes.	Totals.
England and Wales, ...	£10,214,091	£47,113,595	£57,327,686
Scotland, ...	1,137,001	7,688,940	8,825,941
Ireland, ...	571,678	7,183,323	7,755,001
Totals,	£11,922,770	£61,985,858	£73,908,628

It requires no laborious argument to establish from the foregoing
figures first, that the relative means of each of these realms to pay
other imperial taxes can be more closely approximated by measuring
the relative yield of each to the income tax than by any other
process open to our adoption.

Now let me point out what the above figures establish. They
prove that for *England* (so terming England and Wales) her other
imperial taxes are not equal to *five* times her income tax ; that for
Scotland her other imperial taxes do not equal *seven* times her
income tax ; but for *Ireland* her other imperial taxes considerably exceed *twelve* times her income tax.

The pamphlet made a great impression on leading
Liberal statesmen, more particularly on Mr. Childers,
and contributed to deepen the growing belief in England
that the oft-reiterated Irish complaints against excessive
taxation were not without foundation.

CHAPTER XXV.

A.D. 1890-94.

MR. THOMAS SEXTON.

MR. JOHN E. REDMOND ASKS FOR AND OBTAINS THE APPOINTMENT OF A ROYAL COMMISSION.

ON 20th May, 1890, Mr. Thomas Sexton, in the debate
on the *Customs and Inland Revenue Bill*, inquired if the
Chancellor of the Exchequer, before he levied this

increased duty, which would affect Ireland in a particularly burdensome manner, had asked himself whether
the Irish contribution to the revenue was not already
enough. For the last forty years Ireland, a country of
decreasing population and of decreasing capacity to
bear fiscal burdens, had been the victim of a long and
steady course of the most wanton fiscal aggression. In
England the consumption of wine, beer, and spirits was
6¾ gallons per head ; in Scotland it was 4½ gallons
per head ; and in Ireland it was only 3 gallons per head.
If the taxation were fair, it would bear some relation to
the consumption. In England it was 14s. 1d. ; in
Scotland it was 18s. 10d. ; and in Ireland it was 13s.
per head, whereas it really should have been—in
England, 14s. 1d.; in Scotland, 9s. 4d.; and in Ireland,
6s. 3d. He protested against the mean, aggressive, and
disgraceful fiscal policy which weighed down the two
poorer members of the imperial partnership for the
benefit of the richer party. He asked had the Chancellor of the Exchequer formulated any principle with
regard to the relative capacity of the countries which
were partners in the United Kingdom to contribute to
the common purse. The contribution of England to
the imperial revenue, judged by the four direct taxes of
probate, licences, stamps, and income tax, was light.
She contributed 81 per cent. of the whole revenue. On
probate she contributed 87 per cent. ; on licences, 86 per
cent. ; on stamps, 89 per cent. ; and on income tax, 87 per
cent. Ireland's contribution to the imperial revenue
was 8 per cent. On probate duty it was 4½ per cent. ;
on licences, 4·7 per cent. ; on stamps, 3·7 per cent. ; and
on income tax, 4·4 per cent. Judged by these four tests,
Ireland's contribution to the imperial revenue was
double what it ought to have been. He claimed a
select committee, as a matter of right, to consider the
incidence of imperial taxation, and he asked the House

to suspend the proposal for the increased taxation of
Ireland until the committee had reported whether the
present taxation of Great Britain and Ireland was tolerable and fair, and what steps should be taken, if the
Irish burden were found to be undue, to reduce the
contribution to such an amount as would appear to be
a more just contribution from the relative capacity of
each country to the common purse of the United
Kingdom.

Mr. Goschen, in reply to Mr. Sexton, said he thought
he was prepared to grant an inquiry into the financial
relations of the two countries. He would not pledge
himself further without consulting his leader (Mr. W.
H. Smith, First Lord of the Treasury), but he would be
prepared to throw as much light as possible on the
financial relations of the two countries. If inquiry
showed that injustice had been done to any part of the
United Kingdom, steps would be taken to afford redress.
In the debate which followed on that and the succeeding
day, Mr. John Dillon and Mr. T. M. Healy took part.
Mr. Dillon said he was glad that there was to be an
inquiry, and that it would have the best possible results ;
and Mr. Healy asked would the committee be nominated
on party lines or of financial experts. No inquiry had
taken place since that by General Dunne's committee
thirty years ago.

On the 14th July and on the 1st August, Mr. Sexton
asked Mr. Goschen what steps he intended to take for
the appointment of the Select Committee on the Financial Relations of the Three Kingdoms. On 12th August
Mr. Goschen, in reply to Mr. Sexton and Mr. T. W.
Russell, said that it was desirable to have a meeting of
the Committee on Financial Relations that session, in
order that they might consider what line the inquiry
would take, and what information would be required
from the departments. The terms of reference to the

committee were announced on the 13th August as
follows :—

That a select committee be appointed to consider the present
financial relations between England, Scotland, and Ireland, and to
report—

(1) The amount and proportion of revenue contributed to the
Exchequer by the people of England, Scotland, and Ireland respectively :

(2) The amount and proportion of revenue which, under recent
legislation, is paid to local authorities in England, Scotland, and
Ireland respectively :

(3) The amount and proportion of moneys expended out of the
Exchequer (*a*) upon civil and local government services for the
special use of and (*b*) upon collection of revenue in England,
Scotland, and Ireland respectively :

(4) The amount and proportion of State loans outstanding, and
of State liabilities incurred for local purposes in England, Scotland, and Ireland respectively :

(5) How far the financial relations established by the sums so
contributed, paid, advanced, or promised, or by any other existing
conditions, are equitable, having regard to the resources and population of England, Scotland, and Ireland respectively.

A discussion took place on these terms of reference,
in which Mr. T. M. Healy, Mr. Thomas Sexton, and
Mr. Arthur O'Connor took part. Mr. Sexton said of
the reference that it was " in part irrelevant, in part
too restricted, and in part misleading."

The committee nominated consisted of twenty-one
members, of whom four were Irish—Mr. T. W. Russell,
Mr. Thomas Sexton, Mr. John Dillon, and Mr. Arthur
O'Connor. They met once, and ordered some returns
to be printed.

Early in the next session, on 27th February, 1891,
Sir Thomas Esmonde asked the First Lord of the
Treasury to state when the Committee of Inquiry into
the Financial Relations between Ireland and Great
Britain would commence its investigations.

Mr. Goschen replied that he was anxious to push the

matter forward, and would immediately take measures
to have the committee re-appointed.

Mr. Sexton thanked him, and Sir Joseph N. M'Kenna
asked that additional Irish members should be added,
to which Mr. Goschen did not assent.

Again, on 27th April, 1891, Sir Thomas Esmonde
asked when the committee would sit.   Mr. Goschen
replied that the Government and Opposition members
were ready, and that the committee would be appointed
as soon as the Irish members gave notice of the names.
Mr. T. Sexton called attention to the inconvenience of
the delay arising from the non-appointment of the committee, and Mr. Goschen replied that he would put the
committee on the paper.

On 11th June, Mr. Sexton asked how the Exchequer
contribution of £40,000 per year in aid of local taxation
was calculated, and Mr. Goschen replied that it was on
the Probate Duty basis.

On 18th June Mr. H. H. Fowler asked the Chancellor
of the Exchequer when he intended to move for the
Committee on Financial Relations.   Mr. Goschen, in
reply, said it had been put down twice, but could not
be taken after 12 o'clock, owing to objections by Welsh
members.   He hoped he would move it that evening.

On 22nd June Mr. Goschen moved for the appointment of the committee, but the Welsh members again
objected.   In the course of the discussion, Mr. Goschen
made use of the expression—" separate fiscal entity."

Again, on 23rd June, Mr. Goschen moved, and the
Welsh members repeated their objections.

On 9th July Mr. Thomas Sexton moved the reduction
of the Chancellor of the Exchequer's salary by £1,000,
to call attention to the non-appointment of the Committee on Financial Relations.   The Irish contribution
to the Imperial revenue was a scandalous and intolerable
grievance.   Ireland was paying her double share to the

I

Imperial revenue. He was prepared to advance proofs that Ireland was paying £3,000,000 a year to the Imperial revenue more than she should pay. The other Irish members who took part in the debate were Colonel Nolan and Mr. T. P. O'Connor. The motion was defeated by 154 votes to 94.

In the session of 1892 the Government was frequently asked when the special committee would be appointed. The reply was invariably given that the Government was willing to move the appointment, but the Welsh members or the 12 o'clock rule stood in the way. Finally, on the 12th May, Mr. Goschen moved the appointment of the committee. The Welsh members sought to have Wales specifically included, but Mr. Goschen objected, and said—

We cannot agree to accept Wales in this inquiry as a separate financial entity in our fiscal system.

It being midnight, the debate stood adjourned, and the committee was never appointed.

On 8th August, 1892, Mr. J. E. Redmond, in the debate on the address after the change of Government, said :—

There is one portion of the Home Rule scheme which, when we come to discuss it in this House, will probably prove the *crux* of the whole business. I mean the financial portion of it. But it would be manifestly absurd for me, on an occasion such as this, to enter into that. All I will say is, that the financial portion of the scheme of 1886 was never accepted by the late Mr. Parnell, who always made a reservation to the effect that he would endeavour in committee to deal with and amend it. Further than that, I believe the experience of the last six years has convinced many men that the financial arrangements proposed in the Bill of 1886 were unjust to Ireland, and would probably, if passed into law, have resulted in the bankruptcy of the country before many years had elapsed.

On 10th February, 1893, on the motion of Mr. J. J. Clancy, a "return showing for the years ending 31st

March, 1890, 1891, and 1892 respectively (1) the amount
contributed by England, Scotland, and Ireland respectively to the revenue collected by the imperial officers ;
(2) the expenditure on English, Scottish, and Irish services met out of such revenue," was ordered.

Frequent questions on financial relations were asked
in the early part of the session of 1893, and on the
22nd June Mr. Gladstone explained the revised financial
clauses of the Government of Ireland Bill.   On the 3rd
July Mr. Provand, member for the Blackfriars Division
of Glasgow, asked for the re-appointment of Mr.
Goschen's Select Committee to inquire into the Financial Relations of Great Britain and Ireland; and in the
discussion which arose, Mr. J. E. Redmond put the
following question :—

> May I ask whether, in view of the fact that the new financial
> scheme is of a provisional character, the right honourable gentle-
> man will consider the advisability of issuing some tribunal such as
> a Royal Commission to investigate the financial relations between
> the two countries, so that, at the end of the provisional time con-
> templated, the House will be in a position to know with some
> degree of accuracy what the proper contribution of Ireland to the
> imperial expenses should be ?

On 13th July Mr. J. E. Redmond again asked :—

> I beg to ask the First Lord of the Treasury (Mr. W. E. Glad-
> stone) whether he will appoint a Royal Commission to inquire into
> the financial relations between England and Ireland since 1800,
> with a view of fixing the permanent contribution of Ireland to the
> Imperial Exchequer on a just and equitable basis after the establish-
> ment of an Irish Parliament.

In reply Mr. Gladstone said :—

> I have given much attention to this question.   I am aware that,
> for the purpose of fixing definitely the financial relations of the two
> countries, the present information available is insufficient, and it
> follows, of course, that the subject ought to be probed to the
> bottom, and all possible information acquired for the purpose.
> Undoubtedly the Government think the best means of acquiring

that information would be by a Royal Commission ; and it is, therefore, the intention of the Government that Her Majesty shall be
advised to issue a Commission to inquire and report into the
question.

Mr. Goschen intervened to know if Mr. Gladstone
would go back to 1800, or confine himself to the general
proposition of inquiry into the present financial relations
of England and Ireland and those of the immediate
past. Mr. Gladstone thought it best that the inquiry
should commence with the Union.

A most important discussion took place on the 27th
July, 1893, on an amendment moved by Mr. Sexton to
one of the financial clauses of the Home Rule Bill, which
contained a proposal for the appointment of a committee
to regulate Irish finance during an intermediate period.
Mr. Sexton wished to entrust this committee with the
work of inquiring and reporting on Irish relative capacity
to contribute to imperial charges. Mr. Gladstone said
he did not think the committee was one well qualified
to conduct a large and searching inquiry such as should
take place. He considered that a Royal Commission
would be better suited, and urged Mr. Sexton to with-
draw his amendment. In reply to Mr. Goschen, who
said that the committee would be better for ascertaining
principles, and a Royal Commission for ascertaining
facts, Mr. Gladstone said :—

In my opinion, the sole and undivided responsibility for determining principles in connection with charges to be allocated in the
ultimate arrangements between England and Ireland must rest with
Parliament. In the first place, we must give unbounded powers of
inquiry into the facts ; and if we give the Commission that power,
it will be impossible to prohibit the Commission from suggesting to
the Queen, to the Government, and Parliament the inferences
which may appear to arise out of the facts. I do not see how that
can be shut out. It never has been shut out. But no power of
the responsible executive Government can be made over to a Commission. I should certainly, in order that the inquiry may be

conducted with adequate weight, desire to see various interests and classes represented. I should desire, for instance, to see what are called the propertied and privileged classes to see the classes connected with the land—represented. I think a Commission would be an official instrument. But the greatest care must be taken to avoid the possibility of a suspicion that the Commission is to take out of the hands of Parliament any portion of its duties or responsibilities.

Mr J. E. Redmond said that a case was made out for a Commission, and that both sides desired one. A Commission would go on, even though the Home Rule Bill did not become law.

Mr. T. W. Russell said that, whether Home Rule was granted or not, a Commission to inquire into the financial relations of the two countries would be useful. Mr. Redmond had asked for and obtained a Commission, and now Mr. Sexton asked for a committee to inquire into a question which Mr. Redmond had already been promised would be inquired into by a Commission. Finally Mr. Sexton withdrew his amendment by leave.

On the 1st September Mr. Redmond asked Mr. Gladstone when the Government proposed to issue the Royal Commission on Financial Relations, and Mr. Gladstone, in reply, said it would be properly issued early in the next year.

On the 1st December Mr. Gladstone said, in reply to Mr. Sexton, that the Royal Commission would issue early next year, and that the terms of reference would be sufficiently comprehensive.

Mr. Redmond, Mr. Hayden, and Mr. J. J. Clancy, asked on nine or ten subsequent occasions when the appointment of the Commission would take place, and ultimately the Royal Warrant was issued on 24th March, 1894.

CHAPTER XXVI.

A.D. 1894-95-96.

THE ROYAL COMMISSION.

IT would be difficult to gather together for the inquiry men more distinguished in the realm of finance than those selected. Mr. Childers, Lord Farrer, Lord Welby, Sir Robert G. C. Hamilton, and Sir David M. Barbour had all long and honourable careers in the public service, and owed their rank to the faithful and capable discharge of onerous duties in regulating, during the greatest period of expansion, the finances of important Government departments. No less successful in the management of the finances of great banks were the O'Conor Don, Sir Thomas Sutherland, Mr. B. W. Currie, Mr. Charles E. Martin, and Mr. Henry F. Slattery. They had all the knowledge and experience which fall to the lot of directors of these great institutions. Mr. Thomas Sexton had shown himself a capable financier in the conversion of the municipal debt of Dublin ; and Mr. Blake had been Treasurer to the Law Society of Canada. Mr. Childers, Lord Farrer, Sir David Barbour, and Mr. Hunter were all writers of admitted eminence on economic and historical subjects ; whilst Mr. Childers, Lord Welby, Sir Robert Hamilton, the O'Conor Don, the Hon. Edward Blake, Mr. B. W. Currie, Mr. J. E. Redmond, and Mr. Thomas Sexton had all experience in investigation, having served with distinction on Parliamentary Committees or Royal Commissions. A sketch of each member of the Commission will reveal its high character even more conspicuously.

The Right Honourable Hugh Culling Eardley Childers, who was first chairman of the Commission, was born in London in 1827. Graduating at Trinity College, Cambridge, in 1850, he went to Australia in that year. He soon became a member of the recently established Government of Victoria, and held office till 1857, when he returned to England as Agent-General for that colony. He at once proceeded to his M.A. degree at Cambridge, and became a student at Lincoln's Inn. He entered Parliament as Member for Pontefract in 1860. He served with great credit on two select committees—the first on Transportation, in 1861 ; the second on Penal Servitude, in 1863. He was one of the Royal Commissioners who investigated the Constitution of the Law Courts in 1869. He held office as Lord of the Admiralty, 1864-65 ; Financial Secretary of the Treasury, 1865-66 ; Lord of the Admiralty, 1868-71 ; Chancellor of the Duchy of Lancaster, 1872-73 ; Secretary of State for War, 1880-82 ; Chancellor of the Exchequer, 1882-85 ; Home Secretary, 1886. He was the author of pamphlets on *Free Trade, Railway Policy*, and *National Education*. When not holding office, he was a director of some of the great banking, insurance, railway, and steamship companies. He was at all times more a man of business than an orator or debater, and possessed the highest qualifications of ability, erudition, sense of duty, and experience. He was in every way qualified to guide the deliberations of the Royal Commission on the Financial Relations of Great Britain and Ireland. He died on 29th January, 1896.

Reginald Earle, Lord Welby, born in 1832, was educated at Eton and Trinity College, Cambridge. He entered the Treasury in 1856 ; was Private Secretary to the Financial Secretary of the Treasury, 1859-61 ; Head of the Finance Department, 1871-81 ; Auditor of the Civil List, 1881-85 ; Permanent Secretary to the Treasury, 1885-94, on retiring from which he was raised to the peerage. He was chairman of the Royal Commission on Indian Military and Civil Expenditure.

Thomas Henry, Baron Farrer, born in 1819, was educated at Eton and Balliol College, Oxford ; was called to the bar in 1844 ; Assistant Secretary of the Marine Department of the Board of Trade in 1850 ; and Permanent Secretary of the Board of Trade, 1862 to 1886. His published works are *A Memorandum showing the Alterations which would be made in the Present Law by the Enactment of the Merchant Shipping Act*, 1870; *Free Trade versus Fair Trade ; The State in its Relation to Trade ; Gold Credit versus Prices.* The *Times* of 3rd June, 1893, says of him :—" The claims of Sir Thomas Farrer to new honours will be gladly admitted, even by his most pronounced political opponents. He has always shown himself a stout party man, so far as the limits of his official position would allow, and perhaps at times a little further ; but he is a thinker and writer of acknowledged ability, who has served the nation long and well. It is, by the way, a little curious that he should be selected for new dignities at a time when he is manifestly growing a trifle restive at the economic vagaries of some of the ' advanced ' school of London Progressives. He has always been a good Radical, but a good Radical of the school which cannot get over the fundamental fact that two and two make four, and that no amount of sentimental ' gush ' will turn them into five."

For a life of the O'Conor Don see page 48. He was a director of the National Bank of Ireland.

Sir David Miller Barbour, K.C.S.I., born in 1841, was educated at the Queen's College, Belfast ; entered the Bengal Civil Service in 1863 ; was Secretary to the Government of India in the Finance and Commerce Department, 1873 to 1887 ; member of the Council of the Governor-General of India, 1887 to 1893. He published in 1886 *The Theory of Bimetallism and the Effects of the Partial Demonetization of Silver on Eng-*

land and India. He is a recognised authority on Indian finance.

Sir Robert George Crookshank Hamilton, born in 1836, was educated at Aberdeen University. His father was a first cousin to Lord Macaulay. He entered the Civil Service in 1855 as temporary clerk to the War Office. He was soon sent as a commissariat clerk to the Crimea. After his return he was appointed to a clerkship in the Office of Works, where he became known to the Treasury. In 1861 Mr. Lowe, who was Vice-President of the Education Department, selected him to take charge of education finance. In 1869 he was placed at the head of the financial branch of the Board of Trade. The recent extension of the work of the Board of Trade necessitated the employment of an acknowledged financial expert. In 1878 he was made Accountant-General of the Navy, and in 1882 Permanent Secretary of the Admiralty. He was Under-Secretary for Ireland from 1882 to 1886, and Governor of Tasmania from 1886 to 1893. He was Secretary to the Royal Commission of which Sir Lyon Playfair was chairman, which inquired into the organization of the Civil Service. He was a member of the Royal Commission on Colonial Defences, 1881-82, and of the Royal Commission which inquired into the working of the political constitution of Dominica in 1893. He died on 22nd April, 1895. *The Freeman's Journal Record* says of him:—" Evidence of his views on one most important question considered by the Commission was given by Sir Robert Giffen. He was strongly opposed to the view that, in considering the taxation of Ireland, the country should be held responsible for imperial expenditure, or what the Treasury terms ' local services.' It is well known that during his Irish Secretaryship he made strong recommendations on the extravagance of the cost of civil government in Ireland as administered

by imperial officials. In a signed article published in
The Speaker he pointed out that, under imperial control,
the cost of the administration of the law has become so
extravagant that there is an average of £700 a year legal
patronage for every practising barrister in Ireland."

Sir Thomas Sutherland, K.C.M.G., LL.D., born at Aberdeen in 1834, was educated at the Grammar School and
University of that city. He entered the service of the
P. and O. Company, and represented that company in
China for some years. He was for several years a
member of the Legislative Council of Hong Kong, and
was one of the founders of the Hong Kong Docks and
the Hong Kong and Shanghai Bank. He is chairman
of the Peninsular and Oriental Steam Navigation Company, a director of the Suez Canal Company, of the City
Bank, of the Bank of Australasia, and is a Chevalier of
the Legion of Honour.

Bertram Wodehouse Currie, born in 1827, was educated
at Eton. He afterwards travelled abroad, and acquired
a mastery of foreign languages. On returning home he
entered his father's banking business. In 1880 he was
appointed to the Board of the Indian Council, from which
he retired in 1895. To his energy, resolution, and sound
business capacity was due the liquidation, in 1890, by
the Bank of England, of the affairs of Messrs. Baring,
though the bills payable by that firm amounted to
£15,750,000. In 1892 he represented England at the
International Monetary Conference at Brussels, and was
High Sheriff of London in that year. In 1893 he was a
member of the committee which, under the presidency
of Lord Herschell, decided on sanctioning the closing of
the Indian Mints to the free coinage of silver, and in 1895
he initiated the Gold Standard Defence Association.
He died on 29th December, 1896.

William Alexander Hunter, born in 1844, was educated
at the University of Aberdeen. Called to the Bar in

1869, he was Professor of Roman Law at University
College, London, from 1869 to 1878. He was Examiner
in Jurisprudence to the University of London from 1879
to 1884. He is the author of a work on Roman Law
which has already become a classic, and has marked
an epoch in the English study of the subject.

Gustav Wilhelm Wolff, born in 1834, was educated at
a private school in Germany and at Liverpool College.
He became a draughtsman in the Queen's Island Works,
Belfast, in 1858, and subsequently a partner in the great
shipbuilding firm of Harland and Wolff.

John Edward Redmond, born in 1856, was educated at
Clongowes Wood and Trinity College, Dublin ; entered
Gray's Inn, June, 1880 ; was called to the Bar there in
1886, and to the Irish Bar in 1887. He has represented
Irish constituencies in Parliament since 1881. He was
a member of the Royal Commission on the Irish Land
Laws.

Thomas Sexton, born in Waterford in 1848, was
educated in that city. Became a writer on *The Nation*
newspaper in 1869. He was High Sheriff of Dublin
in 1887, and Lord Mayor in 1888 and 1889. He con-
verted the debt of Dublin, and thereby effected considerable economy in the city finances. He was in
Parliament from 1880 to 1895.

The Honourable Edward Blake, born in 1833, was
educated at the University of Toronto. Called to the
Bar in 1856, he was President and Treasurer of the Law
Society of Upper Canada in 1879. He was Chancellor
of the University of Toronto in 1876 ; Premier of
Ontario, 1871-72 ; and Minister of Justice, 1875-77. He
was elected to the Imperial Parliament for South Long-
ford in 1892.

Mr. Charles E. Martin is Deputy-Governor of the Bank
of Ireland.

Mr. Henry F. Slattery was Chairman of the National
Bank of Ireland.

The terms of reference were :—To inquire into the financial relations between Great Britain and Ireland, and their relative taxable capacity, and to report :—

1. Upon what principles of comparison, and by the application of what specific standards, the relative capacity of Great Britain and Ireland to bear taxation may be most equitably determined.

2. What, so far as can be ascertained, is the true proportion, under the principles and specific standards so determined, between the taxable capacity of Great Britain and Ireland.

3. The history of the financial relations between Great Britain and Ireland at and after the legislative Union, the charge for Irish purposes on the Imperial Exchequer during that period, and the amount of Irish taxation remaining available for contribution to imperial expenditure ; also the imperial expenditure to which it is considered equitable that Ireland should contribute.

The witnesses examined were :—Mr. Herbert H. Murray, C.B., Chairman of the Board of Customs ; Mr. Thomas J. Pittar, Principal of the Statistical Office of the Board of Customs; Mr. Alfred Milner, Chairman of the Board of Inland Revenue; Sir Edward W. Hamilton, K.C.B., Assistant Secretary to the Treasury; Mr. Henry A. Robinson, Commissioner of the Local Government Board for Ireland; Sir Joseph M'Kenna ; Dr. T. W. Grimshaw, Registrar-General of Ireland ; Mr. William L. Micks, Secretary to the Congested Districts Board for Ireland ; Mr. John Chaloner Smith, President of the Institute of Civil Engineers in Ireland ; Most Rev. Dr. O'Donnell, Bishop of Raphoe, and member of the Congested Districts Board, Ireland ; Mr. W. P. O'Brien, C.B., formerly Poor Law Inspector and Local Government Inspector, and Vice-Chairman of General Prisons Board, and Assistant Royal Commissioner on Labour ; Sir

Richard H. Sankey, K.C.B., C.E., Chairman of the Board of Public Works, Ireland; Mr. Murrough O'Brien, Member of the Land Commission, Ireland ; Mr. John G. Barton, Commissioner of Valuation, Ireland ; Mr. W. F. Bailey, Assistant Commissioner, Irish Land Commission ; Mr. G. F. Howe, Surveyor of Taxes ; Mr. E. J. Harper, Surveyor to the London County Council ; Sir Robert Giffen, K.C.B., LL.D., Controller-General to the Commercial, Labour, and Statistical Department of the Board of Trade ; and Mr. Thomas Lough, Member of Parliament for West Islington.   The Commission made a most exhaustive examination.

CHAPTER XXVII.

A.D. 1896-97.

REPORT OF THE ROYAL COMMISSION.

EFFECT IN IRELAND.

IN the autumn of 1896 the Royal Commission completed its labours and issued its reports.

Of the thirteen surviving Commissioners, eleven (the O'Conor Don, Lord Farrer, Lord Welby, Mr. Blake, Mr. Currie, Mr. Hunter, Mr. Martin, Mr. Redmond, Mr. Sexton, Mr. Slattery, and Mr. Wolff) signed a joint report, setting forth the following conclusions :—

" (1) That Great Britain and Ireland must, for the purpose of this inquiry, be considered as separate entities.

" (2) That the Act of Union imposed upon Ireland a burden which, as events showed, she was unable to bear.

" (3) That the increase of taxation laid upon Ireland

between 1853 and 1860 was not justified by the then existing circumstances.

"(4) That identity of rates of taxation does not necessarily involve equality of burden.

"(5) That whilst the actual tax revenue of Ireland is about one-eleventh of that of Great Britain, the relative taxable capacity of Ireland is very much smaller, and is not estimated by any of us as exceeding one-twentieth."

Eight separate reports were added, including one each by the two dissentient Commissioners, Sir David Barbour and Sir Thomas Sutherland.

The phrase in the first conclusion of *separate entity* gave rise to much discussion. Mr. Goschen, when Chancellor of the Exchequer, on 22nd June, 1891, denied that Wales was a *separate fiscal entity* when moving the appointment of a select committee to inquire into the financial relations of England, Ireland, and Scotland.

The second conclusion was only another version of that of the Parliamentary Committee of 1815, which reported that the debt and taxation of Ireland after the Union was *a burden which experience has proved too great.*

The third conclusion was reiterated by Irishmen, both in and out of Parliament, from 1853 onwards. Successive Governments, whether Liberal or Conservative, either denied or ignored it.

The fourth conclusion enunciates a canon of international taxation which was a necessary answer to Mr. Gladstone's doctrine of equalized taxation. This canon is foreshadowed in the writings of the O'Conor Don, but was stated with unmistakable clearness by Sir Joseph M'Kenna :—

The fallacy which underlay all his (Mr. Gladstone's) reasoning was the assumption that *identity of imposts* on articles consumed in

Great Britain and Ireland was equivalent to *equality of taxation* of the two countries. It would dignify that assumption to describe it as a sophism. . . . Proclaiming the principle of equality of taxation, he substituted for real equality the spurious device of identical imposts.

The fifth conclusion states the proportion of Irish over-taxation. The several reports contain a concrete estimate for the financial year 1893-94. Ireland contributed, according to Mr. Childers,

in round numbers, about two and three-quarter millions in excess of that which she would have contributed if taxed according to her relative taxable capacity;

and this was adopted by the O'Conor Don, Messrs. Redmond, Martin, Hunter, and Wolff.

According to Lord Farrer, Lord Welby, and Mr. B. W. Currie—

She contributed about two and a-half millions more than she would have contributed if taxed according to what we believe to be her relative taxable capacity.

According to Sir David Barbour, one of the two dissentient Royal Commissioners—

Ireland paid about two and three-quarter millions sterling more than she would have paid if the total revenue taken from her had been in proportion to her " taxable capacity."

Messrs. Sexton, Blake, and Slattery found that the proportion of Irish to British taxable capacity was as 1 to 36.

The publication of these findings, clothed with all the authority of a Royal Commission, found Ireland bled as white as veal by excessive taxation. Mr. Arthur Balfour's academic declaration at Alnwick on 20th July, 1895, that the poverty of Ireland was in part the work of England and Scotland, expressed a truth whose far-reaching character he can have scarcely realized, and for the reparation of which, it is not evident whether it be the will or the power that he lacks.

Since 1853 Ireland had been a battle-ground whereon was waged a long series of political, religious, and social wars. Domestic events had so thoroughly widened the breach between classes, that scarcely a bond remained on which to unite them, save the common ruin which has overwhelmed all. This makes the memorable protests of 1896-97 all the more remarkable. Her Majesty's Lieutenants of Cork, Sligo, Dublin, Limerick, Roscommon, Louth, Wexford, Carlow, Kildare, Galway, Meath, Kerry, and Donegal, in compliance with requisitions, called public meetings, which were attended by all classes of the community. Resolutions were unanimously adopted at these meetings, of which those passed at Cork are here set out as representative of all :—

(1) That this meeting of the taxpayers of the City and County of Cork hereby expresses its sense of the enormous national importance of the findings of the Royal Commission on the Financial Relations of Great Britain and Ireland, and declares its belief that the future prosperity of Ireland and the social happiness and welfare of her people are vitally concerned in securing such a re-adjustment of the present system of taxation as will give effective relief to the Irish taxpayer from a burden which that report conclusively proves to be excessive and unfair.

(2) That it is the duty of the Government to take immediate steps to give effect by remedial legislation to the conclusions suggested by the report of the Royal Commission.

(3) That we call upon the Irish Parliamentary representatives of all shades of political opinion to give to the question of the excessive taxation of Ireland the prominence which its importance deserves, and to press it as a united national demand.

(4) That the Earl of Bandon and proposers and seconders of the foregoing resolutions be appointed a permanent committee (with power to add to their number) to watch the progress of this movement, and to take such action as may be necessary to ensure its success; and that copies of these resolutions be forwarded to the Lord Lieutenant of Ireland, the Chancellor of the Exchequer, the First Lord of the Treasury, the Chief Secretary to the Lord Lieutenant, and the leaders of the Irish Parliamentary Parties.

Similar resolutions were adopted at most Irish public boards, municipal and poor-law; and Earl Cadogan, Lord Lieutenant of Ireland, thus referred to the character of the movement in a speech delivered at Belfast on 20th January, 1897 :—

I hope my words will be endorsed by everyone present, that there never was a movement in Ireland apparently more unanimous throughout the country, among all sections and parties in the country, and one which has been discussed in various districts and by men of various sympathies in a more calm and temperate and sober spirit, in the history of political controversy. I must say I have been very much struck by the manner in which this movement has been organized and carried out in Ireland. Of course, there have been exceptions to the rule which I have laid down from time to time. We have specimens of the rampant rhetoric of amateur rebels ; we have occasionally heard language which, perhaps, we may regret, and to which we do not attach any undue importance ; but taking the meetings throughout the country as a whole, and taking into consideration all I have had an opportunity of reading—perhaps more than any gentleman present—considering all the resolutions passed at these meetings, it is impossible to deny that the attitude of the Irish people at this time, the manner in which they are pressing their desires and wishes. has been such as to leave nothing to desire, and, further, to render it imperative on the Government and Parliament to inquire into and discuss this matter, which is regarded with such universal interest in Ireland.

The columns of *The Times* for the months of December, 1896, and January, February, March, 1897, contain a long array of correspondence from Lord Castletown, the Earl of Dunraven, Lord Farrer, Mr. Bagwell, Professor E. P. Culverwell, F.T.C.D., Mr. Malcolm Inglis, Sir Joseph M'Kenna, Mr. Robert Sanders, and a host of others, which, taken in connection with a series of special and leading articles, shows unmistakably that the question of Irish taxation monopolized during those months the attention of England. A fierce war of passion, prejudice, hatred, ignorance, cynicism, and criticism was waged round the five majority findings

K

of the Royal Commission. Now that the storm has abated, these findings, uninjured and unimpaired, hold the field.

At the memorable meeting in the Mansion House, Dublin, on the 28th December, 1896, a committee was formed to co-operate with such committees as might be appointed by other cities, counties, and public bodies to secure the success of the movement. This committee met weekly, and on the 9th February, 1897, at a conference of delegates from twenty-seven out of the thirty-two Irish counties, held under the presidency of the Earl of Mayo, the constitution and membership of the committee were much enlarged.

On 16th February, the All-Ireland Committee, for so it came to be named, unanimously passed the following resolution :—

That this committee are of opinion that the Irish Parliamentary representatives of all shades of opinion should hold a conference, and take immediate united action on the question of the over-taxation of Ireland and the proposed Royal Commission ; and that copies of this resolution be sent to all the Irish Members of Parliament.

Correspondence took place, on the 19th, 20th, and 22nd February, between Mr. Patrick O'Brien, M.P., and Captain Donelan, M.P., in which Mr. John Dillon was asked to sign a circular, calling a conference of all Irish members. Mr. Dillon wrote :—

With reference to the proposal you made to me to-day, I beg to say that I shall be prepared to advise my friends to attend any conference of Irish members of the House of Commons which may be arranged to consider the possibility of common action on the over-taxation of Ireland, and the proposed Royal Commission.

The following circular was finally issued on the 25th February, signed by Colonel Saunderson and Messrs. T. M. Healy, Horace Plunkett, and J. E. Redmond:—

In view of the forthcoming debate on the question of the financial relations between Great Britain and Ireland, it has been suggested that a conference of all Irish members should be held, so that an interchange of views should take place upon the matter, it being understood that attendance at such conference does not imply either acquiescence in or disagreement with the findings of the recent Commission. We beg, therefore, to request your attendance at such a conference on Tuesday, the 9th March, at five p.m., in Committee Room No. 12.

The All-Ireland Committee, at a largely attended meeting on the 26th February, passed a resolution approving of the conference.

The conference took place on 9th March, and was attended by sixty-three Irish members. Colonel Saunderson took the chair, and Messrs. Abraham, P. O'Brien, T. B. Curran, and Horace Plunkett were appointed honorary secretaries. A sub-committee, consisting of Colonel Saunderson, Mr. T. M. Healy, Mr. J. J. Clancy, and Mr. W. E. H. Lecky, was appointed. Fifty-one Irish members attended the second meeting on the 13th March. Colonel Saunderson again took the chair. Mr. J. J. Clancy read the resolution adopted by the sub-committee:—

That the findings of the Royal Commission on the Financial Relations between Great Britain and Ireland disclose a disproportion between the taxation of Ireland and its taxable capacity as compared with the other parts of the United Kingdom which deserves the immediate attention of Parliament.

This did not meet with the unanimous approval of the conference, which separated after passing a hearty vote of thanks to the chairman.

In the meantime a deputation from the All-Ireland Committee was received by the Chancellor of the Exchequer on the 5th March. The deputation consisted of the Lord Mayor of Dublin; Sir Joseph N. M'Kenna, D.L.; Mr. Simon Mangan, Her Majesty's

Lieutenant for County Meath; Count Plunkett, Barrister-
at-Law ; Mr. R. Keating Clay, J.P., Solicitor, Chairman
of the Dalkey Town Commissioners; Captain Loftus
Bryan, D.L., Wexford; Alderman M. M. Murphy, Solicitor,
Kilkenny ; Mr. More O'Ferrall, D.L., Kildare; Major
Johnson, J.P., Chairman of the Glenties Union ; Mr. James
Ross, J.P., Edgeworthstown ; the Hon. Martin Morris,
J.P., High Sheriff, Galway; Mr. W. H. Cobbe, J.P., Chair-
man, Mountmellick Guardians; Alderman Hadden, J.P.,
Wexford; Mr. P. O'Conor, Barrister-at-Law, Roscommon ; Mr. Daniel J. Wilson, Barrister-at-Law; and
Alderman Sir Robert Sexton, D.L., Dublin.   The depu-
tation was introduced by the Right Honourable Horace
Plunkett, and was authorized by the All-Ireland Committee to call the attention of the Chancellor of the
Exchequer to the over-taxation of Ireland disclosed by
the Royal Commission, and if he expressed any views in
favour of further inquiry, to object to the appointment
of a second Royal Commission.

CHAPTER   XXVIII.

A.D. 1897.

THE ATTITUDE OF THE GOVERNMENT.

"THE TIMES" of 29th December, 1896, declared that
Parliament was the sole authority which should settle
the taxation of Ireland :—

We have contended, surely not without reason, that issues of such
vital importance to the whole population of the United Kingdom
should be determined by no authority less than Parliament itself.

Mr. Goschen, with the concurrence of his chief, in the
Ministry of 1869, stated that the Government would

not refer the *policy* affecting taxation to a Royal Commission. Mr. Gladstone approved of that then, and repeated his approval in the debates of 1893. The attitude assumed by the Government was also condemned by Mr. Goschen in 1869—i.e., proposing the appointment of a Royal Commission, so as to hang up a troublesome question for two or three years.

The Government attitude can be best understood from the following pronouncements.

The Marquis of Lansdowne, Minister for War, in the debate on Lord Castletown's motion in the House of Lords, on 5th March, 1897, said :—

I am not here to contend that, for purposes of statistical comparison, Ireland may not, in one sense of the words, be regarded as a "separate entity." No one will, I suppose, deny that an indiscriminate system of taxation may operate unequally upon different parts of the same country, or that, in the imposition of taxation, a prudent financier should always take care that no tax presses with undue severity upon a particular section of the community, whether that section be represented by a class or by a geographical area ; nor will it be disputed that, when the limits within which the class is distributed coincide with a well-defined geographical area, the inequality, if there is one, becomes more marked, and the sense of wrong more acute. These considerations must obviously apply with peculiar force in the case of Ireland ; and if we mean that the two countries should start with a common system of taxation, and that we should then, having regard to all these considerations, ask whether that system presses inequitably upon Ireland, we need not, I think, quarrel with those who describe Ireland as a "separate entity." I would even go further, and say, that to deny to her the position of a "separate entity" in this sense is to fly in the face of facts. Not a year passes without some legislation of special application to Ireland ; and I think that it may fairly be said that, in proportion as her individuality in such respects is a marked individuality, she has a stronger claim to separate consideration for fiscal purposes.

In the debate on Mr. Blake's motion in the House of Commons on 29th March, Sir M. Hicks-Beach, Chancellor of the Exchequer, admitted that the burden imposed on Ireland by the proportionate contribution required by the Act of Union was more than she could bear, and that Irish complaints against the imposition of taxation in 1853 were justified. He showed that there was large expenditure in Ireland, and that such expenditure was a set-off against over-taxation, and declared that further investigation was necessary.

I want an inquiry into it by persons whose verdict may be accepted as conclusive by honourable members below the gangway, as well as by ourselves, and I maintain that it cannot be controverted that this inquiry has formed no part whatever of the work of the late Royal Commission, and that it cannot, as Lord Farrer has suggested, be fairly and properly settled merely by Treasury returns. We desire in this matter to do full justice to the claim of Ireland, aye, and of Scotland, too, under the proviso as to particular exemptions and abatements in the Act of Union : we desire that the facts as to expenditure shall be also carefully investigated ; and when these facts are fully ascertained, when the meaning of that proviso is laid down, and its application to our existing circumstances is shown by a tribunal in whose verdict both sides may have confidence, then I can assure the House it will be our desire to endeavour to do full justice in this matter to the poorest parts of the United Kingdom. But, under this one condition, we will take no step whatever to depart from that system of common taxation which was established in 1817 ; we will do nothing to impair either the financial or the political permanence of the Union between Great Britain and Ireland ; least of all will we give any countenance to the monstrous doctrine that any part of the United Kingdom should be relieved from its fair obligation to contribute to the necessities of the national debt and of the Army and Navy, and to the maintenance of our great empire.

Before the conclusion of the debate Mr. Goschen declared that the cardinal issue to be referred to the new Commission was :—

Whether the sum spent on local purposes in Ireland ought to be treated as a set-off or not. . . . The matter must be looked at as a whole, and we must take the doctrine of set-off as it has been taken previously on various occasions.

He defined the duty of the new Royal Commission as follows :—

First, ought there to be a set-off, and if so, was that properly calculated in the Treasury returns? Secondly, ought there, or ought there not, to be a contribution towards imperial expenses from Ireland? and thirdly, is there anything in the circumstances of to-day that would require the application and giving effect to that part of the Act of Union that requires that under certain circumstances abatements and exemptions are fair to the poorer country?

History again repeated itself. Defeated in the original position it took up, the Government did not think of doing right, but looked around for a new position. Not a single reference in Mr. Goschen's proposed inquiry of 1897 was contained in his references to the select committee of 1890-91-92.

CHAPTER XXIX.

A.D. 1897.

THE PROPOSED NEW COMMISSION.

THE TERMS OF REFERENCE STRONGLY OBJECTED TO.

ON the 11th February, 1897, Mr. A. J. Balfour announced in the House of Commons the terms of reference to the new Royal Commission which the Government proposed to appoint. The "All-Ireland" Committee, which met at the Mansion House, Dublin, on the 12th February, unanimously adopted the following resolutions :—

(1) That this meeting protests against the appointment of a second Commission to further inquire into any matters already inquired into and reported on by the late Royal Commission.

(2) That whilst fully sympathizing with the financial claims of Scotland, we consider that, having regard to

the report of the late Royal Commission, the just claims of Ireland are prior to, and should not be delayed for or complicated with, those of Scotland.

(3) That the terms of reference to the proposed Commission on expenditure common to England, Ireland, and Scotland are most unfair and unjust to Ireland.

At a later stage, in June, the All-Ireland Committee, after consultation with the leading Irish authorities on the question, issued the following memorandum :—

" The All-Ireland Committee urgently presses upon the Irish representatives in Parliament the great importance of demanding a modification of the terms of reference to the new Commission as announced by the Government.

" It is essential to secure that the constitutional relations of Great Britain and Ireland in fiscal matters, provided for in the Act of Union and the Act for the Amalgamation of Exchequers, shall not be left out of consideration by the new Commission, and that this Commission, which is (according to the statement of the Government) to be supplementary to the former one, shall not ignore the question of the comparative wealth and comparative progress of Great Britain and Ireland since the date of the Union, and the fact of the great difference between the taxation borne by Ireland and her taxable capacity.

" It is also urged that the consideration of the case of Ireland should not be retarded by an investigation into the fiscal position of Scotland. The terms of reference to the former Commission were limited to the financial relations between Great Britain and Ireland. If the supplementary Commission is directed to inquire into the case of Scotland, there will be a departure from the scope of the previous inquiry. It is submitted that, if the people of Scotland demand an inquiry into the financial position of their country, this should be the subject of investigation by a separate Commission.

"The Committee further submit that the question of any re-adjustment or reduction of expenditure on Irish services is one to be dealt with by Parliament and the Government as a matter of policy, and cannot be properly considered by a Commission inquiring into the financial relations of Great Britain and Ireland.

" The second proposed term of Government reference would practically involve a prolonged investigation into all the Civil Service and other departments of the State in England, Scotland, and Ireland, and into the position, pay, and duties of the Government officials in the three kingdoms. Again, the expediency of reducing or re-adjusting the expenditure on Irish local services cannot be considered on the grounds of financial advantage alone, without taking into account historical, social, and local influences, which must be weighed before any profitable conclusion can be reached."

The terms of reference to the new Commission proposed by the Government are as follows :—

1. To inquire and report how much of the total expenditure which the State provides may properly be considered to be expenditure common to England, Scotland, and Ireland, and what share of such common expenditure each country is contributing after the amount expended on local services has been deducted from its true revenue.

2. How the expenditure on Irish local services which the State wholly or in part provides compares with the corresponding expenditure in England and Scotland, and whether such Irish expenditure may with advantage be re-adjusted or reduced.

3. Whether, when regard is had to the nature of the taxes now in force, to the existing exemptions, and to the amounts of the expenditure by the State on local services, the provision in the Act of Union between Great Britain and Ireland with regard to particular exemptions or abatements calls for any modification in the financial system of the United Kingdom.

At the convention held in the Mansion House, Dublin, on 22nd April, 1897, the following resolution was passed :—

That this convention further protests against the terms of reference to the new Commission announced by Her Majesty's Government, and condemns them as framed in disregard of Ireland's constitutional rights, and as one-sided, and as relegating to a Commission questions of policy and expediency fit for determination by Parliament alone.

The All-Ireland Committee suggest that the Government terms of reference should be modified as follows :—

1. To inquire and report whether or not it is the true meaning of the Act of Union and the Act for the Amalgamation of the Exchequers that the amount of Exchequer expenditure for civil administration in Ireland, or any, and if so, what part of such expenditure, should be taken into account in considering the relative capacity of Great Britain and Ireland to bear taxation, and the proportion in which such taxation is borne by them respectively.

2. How much of the total expenditure which the State provides may (within the meaning of the Act of Union and the Act for the Amalgamation of the Exchequers) be considered to be expenditure common to Great Britain and Ireland, and what share of such common expenditure each has been and is contributing after the amount expended upon services which (having regard to these statutes) may be considered local services has been deducted from its true revenue.

3. How much of the total expenditure which the State provides for purposes considered as aforesaid common to Great Britain and Ireland has been and is, on an average, actually expended in Great Britain or Ireland respectively.

4. How the expenditure which the State provides in aid of Irish local rates, or in support or aid of services in Ireland, which in Great Britain are supported out of local rates, compares with similar expenditure in Great Britain.

5. Whether, when regard is had to the nature of the taxes now in force, to the existing exemptions, to the comparative wealth of Great Britain and Ireland, to the comparative rate of their national progress, and to the amount of the expenditure by the State as aforesaid in Great Britain or Ireland respectively, the provisions in the Act of Union between Great Britain and Ireland with regard to particular exemptions or abatements call for any modification in the financial system of the United Kingdom, or for the transfer to the Imperial Exchequer of the liability for the support of any services in Ireland at present, wholly or in part, maintained from local rates in Ireland.

" N.B.—The proposed modification of the terms of reference is not to be taken as in any way detracting from the objections entertained to the appointment of any new Commission."

In the debate in the House of Commons on 30th March, 1897, Sir Edward Clarke, Q.C., thus referred to the proposed new Commission :—" The real question in this debate is whether there is to be a further inquiry with regard to certain matters which it is necessary to ascertain. Now, Sir, I believe I can show the House that the appointment of a new Commission is wholly unnecessary. I find in the terms of the reference to the new Commission which has been laid before the House that the first thing it has to do is to inquire and report

How much of the total expenditure for which the State provides may be properly considered expenditure common to England, Scotland, and Ireland, and what share of such common expenditure each country is contributing after the amount expended on local services has been deducted from the true revenue.

There is no doubt that that question indicates matters upon which the Government and Parliament ought to be informed in dealing with this subject. But no one can suggest a single question contained in that paragraph of the reference to the new Commission which has not been fully and completely answered by the officials of the Treasury on the best information they could possibly obtain. The amount of imperial expenditure on Ireland is not a matter of dispute ; the returns are laid before the House every year, and we have the amount of local expenditure in each of the three kingdoms stated in a complete table. Then we are to get the true revenue of each of the three kingdoms ; and the moment you have these figures it is merely a subtraction sum in order to answer the question put in the first reference. Upon these very questions a great amount of labour has already been expended by the representatives of the Treasury."

He then alluded to the Select Committee of 1890;
to the terms of reference to it; to the return presented to the House by Mr. Jackson on the 10th of
July, 1891 (No. 329); to the further return presented
by Sir John Hibbert, the then Secretary to the Treasury, on the 24th of February, 1893, giving the actual
figures to the end of the financial year 1891-92 ; to
the evidence of Sir Edward Hamilton ; and then continued :—

" With the figures supplied from these authoritative
sources it is perfectly easy to calculate the amount of
Ireland's contributions to the imperial expenditure from
the year 1889-90 down to 1896. I will not give the
totals, for the figures are many, but it is easy to take the
result on a percentage. The average contribution of
Ireland to imperial services for that period was 3·44 per
cent. I cannot understand what additional information
the Government can possibly want, or where they are to
go for it. The First Lord of the Treasury said himself
on February 16th :—

As all the information that can be obtained about the estimated
taxation of Ireland and Great Britain was laid before the late Commission, it may be assumed that the new Commission will not find
it necessary to go into that again.

"Now, the figures which show a percentage of contribution to the imperial expenditure of 3·44 have been seized
upon by the opponents of the Irish claim as if they
absolutely disposed of it. The argument is that the
Irish claim to pay taxes in the proportion of one to
twenty, but that, as a matter of fact, they are only contributing to imperial expenditure in the proportion of
one to thirty-two or thirty-three.

" Sir David Barbour says in his report :—

On the assumption that the taxable capacity of Ireland is one-
twentieth of that of the United Kingdom, Ireland paid in 1893-94
about two and three-quarter millions sterling more than she would

have paid if the total revenue taken from her had been in proportion to her taxable capacity. In the same year there was expended for Irish purposes about three and three-quarter millions in excess of what would have been admissible if the expenditure for Irish purposes had also been in proportion to Ireland's "taxable capacity." On the whole account, Ireland may be said to have been a gainer in 1893-94 of about one million sterling ; or, in other words, after meeting the expenditure for Irish purposes, she contributed about one million less towards imperial purposes than she would have done if her contribution for imperial purposes had been in proportion to her "taxable capacity."

" Sir David Barbour seems to think that that disposes of the whole question, and the *Edinburgh* reviewer takes much the same view. But it seems to me that this proportion of one to thirty-two is highly disputable. The representatives of Ireland upon the Commission, it is true, did not greatly resist its acceptance ; they explained that they attached comparatively little importance to it, because in their opinion the calculation was irrelevant. The Irish representatives were, however, perhaps remiss in allowing the figure to pass unchallenged, because there is very good reason for believing that this alleged contribution of only one-thirty-second to the imperial expenditure is a loose calculation altogether. But, if I were objecting to the claim of Ireland in this matter, and refusing to consider her case upon the ground that there was no grievance of this kind, I certainly should not appoint another Commission, for a new Commission will probably examine the figures more exhaustively. We have some means of correcting the calculation ourselves. The distinction between payments for local services and the amounts contributed to the imperial revenue began in 1890, in the reference to the committee then appointed ; and the Treasury, in the report which they then supplied, dealt with 'imperial services, English services, Scotch services, and Irish services,' and said that expenditure on the

National Debt service and expenses incurred under the National Debt Redemption Act, the Naval Defence Fund, Army services, Ordnance services, and Navy services, must be regarded as strictly imperial. They also said that the expenditure charged upon the Consolidated Fund included items which were clearly imperial, or which could not be divided between the three kingdoms. Lord Welby's name appeared upon this paper as that of the Treasury official who supplied the information ; and, of course, Lord Welby was not likely to quarrel with his own classification before the committee. The authority for that classification was found when Sir Edward Hamilton came to be examined, and gave his evidence, which will be found in the second volume of the report of the evidence at page 124. He said that he appeared there as the representative of the Treasury, and he said that he had talked the matter over with his colleagues, and that he was expressing not merely his personal opinion, but that of the Treasury. The declaration of Sir Edward Hamilton was made to the Commission on the 14th of November, 1895, when his superiors at the Treasury, for whom he professed to speak, were the present First Lord of the Treasury (Mr. Balfour) and the present Chancellor of the Exchequer (Sir M. Hicks-Beach). Then he went on to give a history of this classification. He was asked if it was a Treasury classification simply, and his answer was :—

Yes. Mr. Goschen was the original authority for it, and it has been carefully considered since. I do not mean to say that exception may not be taken ; it is a line that is difficult to draw.

" So far as this distribution of figures is concerned, it has so clearly and distinctly the strongest authority of the Treasury, that I do not think Her Majesty's Government can expect that any further investigation of the matter will alter the figures to the detriment of Ireland ; but it might quite possibly alter them the other way. Sir Edward Hamilton in his evidence—Question 10,511 —said the item for the collection of taxes in Ireland was a moot point. Again—Question 10,518—he said the Lord Lieutenant's charge was a moot and doubtful charge. He was pressed with regard to education in the Queen's Colleges, which is a very large item, amounting to a million. That also he thought was a moot charge. Then comes the police. He admitted the proposition that, instead of one and a-half million— £1,439,000 – being charged to Irish expenses, as is done under the calculation with which I have been dealing, a large proportion of it ought to have been charged to imperial expenditure; and if these alterations were made, they would very largely alter the figure with respect to Ireland. In the return of 1891 the figures giving the contribution to imperial expenditure show a percentage of about 3 or 4 per cent. There was an appendix to that return, showing the percentages of expenditure in 1889-90, 1890-91, and 1891-92 on English, Scotch, and Irish services 'after the cost of the police in each of the three kingdoms (so far as that cost is met out of revenue contributed to the Exchequer, or under the Local Taxation Act), and the special grants for light railways and distress works in Ireland, have been deducted from that expenditure.' Who suggested in 1891 that that should be deducted ? Of course, the authorities then in power. Why ? Because it must have occurred to some of them that it was not fair to charge all this against Ireland in her local account, and that a portion at least ought to be deducted. I hope I am making it clear. It brings me to this point. The *Edinburgh* reviewer deals with this question in one of the most interesting passages of his article, and he comes to the conclusion that if you made adjustments which might be reasonable

upon this particular figure, you would deduct from it—
from the local expenditure of Ireland—a sum of three-
quarters of a million ; and he says that that would still
leave Ireland short of the contribution which, according
to her taxable capacity—one in twenty—she ought to
pay. If you make the alteration in the figures and the
allowance which the *Edinburgh* reviewer suggests to be
a fair allowance, you will find that Ireland contributes,
and has contributed, to the imperial expenditure in the
proportion of one in twenty-two, which is very little
indeed short of the full contribution which anybody
suggests that she ought to make. I think there are
other considerations which undoubtedly ought to be
borne in mind; and possibly, if this new Commission is
to be appointed, it would be as well to take some note
of the extent to which the moneys voted by Parliament,
whether for English, Scotch, Irish, or imperial purposes,
are expended within England, Scotland, and Ireland
respectively. I confess I do not think the calculation is
legitimate at all, for reasons which stand apart from this
discussion of the figures; but if you deal with this matter
on the footing that there are three taxable entities or
areas to be considered, and you are endeavouring to
ascertain the burden upon these areas, it is obvious that
the question how much expenditure takes place within
the limits of each area, is a most important question. Of
the money expended on the public service in Ireland, I
should think a good deal comes to England ; but of the
money that is expended on the public service in England,
I am afraid very little flows over to Ireland ; and should
it be thought necessary again to investigate these figures
which we all have at hand, I hope that the Commission
will be entitled to examine what proportion of the sums
voted under each head of expenditure is actually expended in the country to which the account refers. Now,
let me pass at once to the second question stated in

this reference upon Financial Relations. The second question is—

How the expenditure on Irish local services, for which the State wholly or in part provides, compares with the corresponding expenditure in England or in Scotland, and whether such Irish expenditure may with advantage be readjusted or reduced.

Surely we want no Commission about that. There are two questions, and two questions only. The first is, how Irish local expenditure, classified as I have already shown, compares with the local expenditure of England and Scotland. We know it : we have all the figures, and have had them for years, and if there was another Commission to-morrow, the only thing would be for Sir Edward Hamilton to hand in again a copy of the statement which he handed in before, and which gives the whole information on the subject. The other question put is this : whether Irish expenditure may with advantage be readjusted or reduced. Now, really, it seems a little absurd to refer that question to a Commission. The question is not how it should be reduced, but whether it could with advantage be readjusted or reduced. O'Conor Don, the chairman of the late Commission, says in his report that the possibility of reducing it may be a proper subject for a separate inquiry. But it is not a question of the possibility of reducing it. The question put by the Government is, whether it could with advantage be readjusted or reduced. I refer them to page 50 of the report—the report of Lord Farrer and his colleagues, who say :—

We are of opinion that the excessive expenditure of Ireland which we have described, although it may be no justification for the excessive taxation of Ireland, is at once a pecuniary loss to the taxpayers of Great Britain and a cause of demoralization to Ireland.

And no Commission you ever have will recommend more strongly than that the readjustment or reduction of Irish expenditure   But if you want a stronger testi-

L

mony, and from another quarter, I refer you to page 105
of the report of Mr. Sexton. Mr. Sexton contends that
the present cost of administering Ireland is very excessive,
and there says :—

For this flagrant evil of wasteful and disproportionate expenditure there is but one remedy.

"Of course, the remedy that was proposed was one
which goes into the question of political action. But
upon the question whether expenditure in Ireland is excessive, or whether it can with advantage be readjusted
or reduced, that Commission are absolutely clear and
unanimous in their reports. Just let me put this practical consideration to the House. Suppose a new Commission were appointed, and it reported, in answer to
this second paragraph, that the expenditure in Ireland
could with advantage be readjusted and reduced, you
would have learned nothing new, you would have
learned exactly what this Commission has told you.
But suppose the Commission were to report that the
expenditure upon civil government in Ireland was
moderate in amount and reasonable in character, and
that it produced an effective and satisfactory result in
economical and good government, the House would
tear up the report with ridicule. We know the facts
better than that. I know the reason of much of this
extravagant expenditure. Hon. members opposite have
said, so long as this country was dealing with them in
a way which they did not approve of, and incurring expenditure which they did not desire to sanction by their
votes, they were determined to get all they could ; and
as long as they were being taxed so heavily, they meant
to get as much back as they could, and did not mind
very much whether it was the salary of an unnecessary
judge or was expended in any other way. The way
in which this House has dealt with Irish expenditure

has been perfectly grotesque. Last night the Chancellor of the Exchequer said that, if hon. members opposite would assist in making a little reduction in the excessive cost of the judicial establishment in Ireland, he would promise them that they should have full advantage of every shilling of the saving."

Mr. T. M. Healy : " He denied that to-day."

The Chancellor of the Exchequer : " No, I did not. I adhere to every word of that statement. I said I could not deal with matters of the past, and that I was only responsible for matters of the future."

He then referred to the late appointment of an Irish judge, and resumed :—" I would like to call attention to the third paragraph in the terms of reference to the proposed Commission, the words of which are extremely important, I think, because these words do carry with them a most important acknowledgment of the case of the Irish members :—

Whether, when regard is had to the nature of the taxes now in force, to existing exemptions, and to the amount of expenditure by the State on local services, the provision in the Act of Union between Great Britain and Ireland with regard to " particular exemptions or abatements " calls for any modification in the financial system of the United Kingdom.

" Sir, I confess I think that the insertion of those words in that reference is a very important fact. It recognises that the Act of Union is still in force, continued as it was, and having effect given to it, by the Act of 1816, and it acknowledges the right of the Irish people now to come with the Act of Union and the Act of 1816 in their hands, and to claim, if they can show good cause in the circumstances of their country, to have exemptions or abatements. But just let me suggest this, that the question now has passed from the region of Treasury investigation and of financial fact into a region of most controversial discussion of

political matters. I must, in passing, say that I greatly
regretted to hear from the Chancellor of the Exchequer
last night that he proposed to take a judge from England, and one from Scotland, and one from Ireland to
serve on the proposed Commission. I do hope we are
not going on with the practice of withdrawing judicial
officers from their proper work to put them upon Commissions with which they have nothing to do, and upon
which their authority will practically be of no use at all.
It is acknowledged by the terms of this reference that
the Act of Union and the Act of 1816 are still effective
instruments for the protection of Ireland, if the circumstances of Ireland entitle her to claim such protection ;
and what does this House care about the report of one
judge, or of three judges, as to what they say is the
meaning of these words ?   The House of Commons
must construe them for itself, and will construe them,
as I believe, not in a technical or niggardly spirit, but
with the desire to give full effect to the pledge which
was contained in those Acts as to the treatment, and
separate treatment, which Ireland should receive."
    He then mentioned the Marquis of Salisbury's classi-
fication of Royal Commissions, and continued :—
    " If it is only financial fact that is to be obtained, we
do not want a Commission. If the Chancellor of the
Exchequer gave directions to the Treasury officials, he
would have within the next week reports upon all these
points given by persons whose authority would never be
questioned, and he would gain nothing if they were
filtered, as Sir Edward Hamilton's report was, through
the different members of a Royal Commission. If, on
the other hand, we are going to adopt the second kind
of Royal Commission, and to shut up violent persons to
fight out between themselves in the Commission-room
the meaning of the Act of Union and the Act of 1816,
surely it would be far better to let us have the facts stated

before the House, and to let us, here in the House, and not within the limits of a Royal Commission, have these questions fought out. Let me say further, the question now referred to in that third paragraph of the terms of reference is a serious question of policy, and it is not a question of fact at all. We have got all the facts ; the question is whether, in dealing with Ireland, you are entitled to set off the expenditure upon the local services in Ireland against her general contribution. I confess I take the strongest view that you are not. Upon this I would refer specially to the terms of the Act of 1816. It is perfectly clear that the scheme of that Act was that the taxes being imposed, such taxes as Parliament might think right, the produce of those taxes was to come into a common fund, and out of that fund the expenditure was to take place by one authority, which is the authority of this House, and for all the purposes of the empire. To my thinking, the expenditure upon the payment of the police in Ireland is as much an imperial charge, in the true sense of the word, as anything else that appears on our accounts. When I hear these conflicting voices, when I hear it said from that side,

Oh, your expenditure is an imperial expenditure ; when you spend money in Ireland, you are spending money at the direction of the Council of the whole nation, and for purposes which it thinks wise ;

and when, on the other hand, I hear it said,

Oh, you must not consider that as an imperial expenditure ; I am going to look and see how much you cost us ; I am going to make out a balance of account, and see what we are to debit and credit Ireland with—

I ask myself with some wonder,

Which is the Unionist voice?

" If this were truly and properly to be called Irish expenditure, I could see no escape from the conclusion

that it must be governed by Irishmen according to Irish
ideas. It is because I believe that the expenditure
which is under the control of this House, the great
majority here being representatives of Great Britain, is
all imperial expenditure, that I would protest against
the attempt to cut and carve up the accounts with regard
to England and Scotland and Ireland with a debit and
credit account, as if they were mere branches which were
connected together by commercial associations, but were
not part of the one imperial whole. I must say, from
my own point of view, I feel very strongly that while
it is necessary, in order that we may fulfil our treaty
obligations to Ireland, and the obligations we came
under in 1816, that we should carefully regard the condition of Ireland, and endeavour to deal fairly and
generously with her in her need, if need be proved to
exist, we should absolutely refuse to cut up the accounts
of our imperial expenditure because we happen to spend
one sum of money in Ireland, as if Ireland herself had no
separate and exclusive control in it. I would just like
to add, almost in parenthesis, that there is this fatal flaw
about this calculation : you are trying to split the taxation as if it did not matter how large is the taxation you
impose so long as you spend it upon the population
where you raise it. According to that theory we should
be doing Ireland, in her poverty and trouble, no harm at
all if we were to impose three millions more taxes per
annum upon her, always provided that we doubled the
number of her police, and gave her more judges, and, for
the special benefit of the landlords of Ireland, gave her
an army of assistant-commissioners."

This utter pulverization of the pretexts for the appointment of a second Commission, and the exposure of the
irrelevancy and purposeless nature of the proposed
inquiry, seem to have settled the matter, as, after the
lapse of seven months, no Commission has been
appointed.

CHAPTER XXX.

RUINED IRELAND.

THE following is taken from Mr. Murrough O'Brien's memorandum, Appendix II, Volume I, of the Report of the Royal Commission :—

" The misery and moral evils caused by over-taxation, and the misspending of the Irish revenue, cannot be measured in money or expressed in figures." Two of the four economic causes of Ireland's poverty and non-progression in prosperity, as compared with the rest of the United Kingdom, are :—

" (1) Over-taxation for over ninety years.

" (2) Drain of absentee rental.

" The manifest symptoms of this poverty are :—

" (1) A continually diminishing population.

" (2) Decaying towns and villages.

" (3) Emigration.

" (4) Migration of labourers for temporary employment to Great Britain and the United States.

"(5) Annually recurring distress and periodical famines.

" (6) Persistent and unabated social and political discontent.

" (7) The appearance of the mass of the people, their houses, clothes, and food.

" It is doubtful whether Ireland has increased at all in wealth during the last thirty years, although, owing to the diminishing population, it may be shown statistically that there are more acres of land, pounds of valuation, miles of railway, &c., per head of the population ; but this is not prosperity.

" No poor agricultural country such as Ireland could stand the continued drain of excessive taxation she has been subjected to, and of remittances to absentees without the economic effect of such unremunerative payments becoming evident. These payments are equivalent to a perpetual bad harvest or annual cattle plague. If the entire potato crop or the saleable produce of Ireland's live stock were annually carried away without return, or if absentee payments were made in one sum as a tribute, the magnitude of the economic drain would be clearly recognised. The evil is no less because these payments without return are made to a number of individuals, or go to support the dignity, maintain the strength, and reduce the debt of Great Britain."

The following observations by Mr. Charles Booth are taken from Appendix X, Volume II, of the evidence received by the Royal Commission :—

" The view is commonly held that in general well-being Ireland has enormously improved since the famine. No evidence of this improvement is to be found in the occupation returns, which, on the contrary, point to a demoralization of industry likely to be the cause as well as consequence of poverty and waning trade, and certain to be the source of political discontent. I know that figures may be, and are, drawn from bank deposits and other returns, which seem to tell a different story. I shall not attempt to reconcile this conflict of evidence. To do so would be beyond the scope of this paper. I can only state the conclusions to which the census returns point.

" In the picture of desolation which the Irish figures afford there seems little room for delusion. When industries decay, those who have been supported by them cling to their employment as long as possible, . . . and the numbers given include many who no longer find a living in what they profess to do. . . . In such a case the facts are assuredly worse than the figures disclose."

Of *general labourers*, a very numerous class in Ireland, he says :—

" They sprang into existence, not from any need of their services, but as the outcome of agricultural and industrial distress and charitable doles on an enormous scale."

Domestic servants were in 1841, 4·2 per cent. of the population ; in 1881, 8·2 per cent., there being an actual positive increase of 85,000. Mr. Booth remarks :—

" What is the explanation of these remarkable figures? It would be simplest to show they are incorrect ; . . . but I have found no loophole of escape, and the comparison of successive decades shows how gradually the position of Ireland was reversed, from being the most economical to being the most extravagant in domestic service. The only explanation which suggests itself is that servants are more numerous where poverty makes service cheap.

" The decrease in those employed in *agriculture*, though affecting each branch, shows itself, of course, mainly in the labourers and farm servants, who have fallen from 1,326,000 in 1841 to 329,000 in 1881.

" In 1841 there were 72,000 persons occupied in *building:* in 1881 there were but 56,000."

" The total employed at *manufacture* has dropped from 989,000 to 379,000 (or 61·7 per cent.)."

CHAPTER XXXI.

A.D. 1897.

ORGANIZATION.

A CONVENTION was held in the Mansion House, Dublin, on 22nd April, to establish an organization with the object of redressing the over-taxation of Ireland disclosed by the report of the late Royal Commission. The attendance was most representative and influential, and letters of apology were read from leading men in all parts of the country. The Convention was addressed by the Lord Mayor of Dublin, the Earl of Mayo, Mr. R. Keating Clay, J.P., Solicitor ; the Rev. Mr. Finlay, Protestant Dean of Leighlin ; Dean White, P.P., Nenagh ; Professor Culverwell, F.T.C.D. ; Dr. Joseph E. Kenny, Mr. Arthur W. Samuels, Q.C. ; Mr. John Carolan, J.P. ; Mr. J. F. Riordan, Solicitor ; Captain O'Callaghan Westropp, J.P. ; Mr. John Sweetman, Mr. Robert Sanders, J.P. ; and Mr. Richard J. Kelly, Barrister-at-Law. The following resolutions were adopted :—

The Earl of Mayo proposed the first resolution, as follows :—

That this Convention expresses its dissatisfaction with the position taken up by Her Majesty's Government in the recent debate on the financial relations between Great Britain and Ireland, protests against the appointment of the proposed new Commission, and declares that the people of Ireland are determined by every legitimate means to prevent any delay in giving to Ireland the relief to which she has been found entitled.

Professor Culverwell, F.T.C.D., proposed the second resolution, as follows :—

That an organization, to be called the Irish Financial Reform League, be now constituted, with branches in each county and city in Ireland, to further the movement for the redress of the imperial taxation in Ireland, and to maintain the financial rights to which she is constitutionally entitled. That every person who subscribes one shilling a year to this League shall be admitted a member thereof, and that it be referred to the All-Ireland Committee to draw up the basis on which this League shall be founded. That a subscription list be opened, pending the formation of the organization referred to in this resolution, to defray the preliminary expenses which have been already incurred, and the further expenses which must be met in forming this League, and in advancing the objects which the All-Ireland Committee are advocating.

Mr. Samuels, Q.C., proposed the third resolution, as follows :—

That this Convention further protests against the terms of reference to the new Commission announced by Her Majesty's Government, and condemns them as framed in disregard of Ireland's constitutional rights, and as one-sided, and as relegating to a Commission questions of policy and expediency fit for determination by Parliament alone.

Captain O'Callaghan Westropp then proposed the fourth resolution, as follows :—

This Convention demands that there shall be forthwith granted to Ireland relief identical with that conferred upon England by the Agricultural Rating Act of 1896, by which farmers in England are granted from the Imperial Exchequer relief to the extent of one-half the rates payable on their agricultural holdings ; and this Convention calls upon all Irish representatives in Parliament to take steps forthwith to secure that in this respect right be done.

The All-Ireland Committee in due course issued an address to the people of Ireland, and the constitution of the Irish Financial Reform League :—

TO THE PEOPLE OF IRELAND.

In accordance with the resolution passed at the Mansion House Convention on the 22nd April, 1897, the All-Ireland Committee now lay before their fellow-countrymen the Constitution of the Irish Financial Reform League.

It is evident that passing events, both in and out of Parliament, each day proclaim the necessity for, and show the advantage of, united action on the part of all Irishmen to secure the redress of their financial grievances.

They therefore appeal with confidence to the people of Ireland, of all classes and every shade of politics, to support and extend this League throughout the length and breadth of our country, in the full confidence that the significant unanimity hitherto displayed on this question will continue, and, deriving from organization fresh vigour and power, will, in this weighty matter, secure that " right be done."

As the organization of the Irish Financial Reform League, and the conduct of the movement in a systematic and business-like manner, will necessitate considerable expenditure, the All-Ireland Committee consider that the time has come to appeal to their countrymen for that financial support which has hitherto been only asked from and afforded by the members of the committee.

Subscriptions, either direct or through local branches of the Irish Financial Reform League, will be received and acknowledged by the Hon. Treasurers of the League. Cheques and postal orders may be made payable to " Irish Financial Reform League, Mansion House, Dublin."

IRISH FINANCIAL REFORM LEAGUE.

1. That this League be called the " Irish Financial Reform League."

2. The objects of this League are to secure united action on the part of all Irishmen in furthering the movement for the redress of the over-taxation of Ireland, and to maintain the financial rights to which she is constitutionally entitled.

3. Every person favourable to the objects of this League may become a member on the payment of one shilling a year to the funds of the League. On his subscription being received, and his name enrolled in the list of members, a card of membership will be delivered to him, which will entitle him to admission to the general meetings of the League.

4. That the All-Ireland Committee Meeting in Dublin be constituted the Central Body of the League.

5. That representatives be nominated to act on the All-Ireland Committee by local committees of the League, to be formed in the counties, cities, and towns of Ireland.

6. That in the event of there being no local committee, the League shall invite local taxpayers to form a committee.

7. That all subscriptions when received by local committees be forwarded to the " Treasurers, All-Ireland Committee, Mansion House, Dublin," after defraying expenses.

8. That the Lord Mayor of Dublin for the time being and the Earl of Mayo be Treasurers to the Irish Reform League Fund. The moneys received to be lodged by the Treasurers to the credit of the Irish Financial Reform League, at the National Bank, College Green, Dublin.

The organization has been extended to many parts of Ireland, and very influential meetings have been held for that purpose ; amongst others, in Carlow, with the Right Honourable Henry Bruen presiding ; and in Cork, with the Earl of Bandon presiding. At the latter meeting, held on the 2nd November, the O'Conor Don made an earnest appeal to Irishmen to unite on the taxation question. From the day he entered Parliament, thirty-seven years ago, he has been invariably found on the Irish side of this question. He supported General Dunne, Sir Joseph M'Kenna, and Mr. Mitchell Henry when they raised it in Parliament. He voted for General Dunne's Draft Report, and on the death of Mr. Childers was elected Chairman of the Royal Commission. His life is the bridge which joins these two great epochs in the Irish effort for redress. No one recognises more fully than he, who has played his part so honourably and well in the history of the movement, why all the protests of the past have been fruitless, and how vital it is to Ireland that the justice which he has seen so long delayed should be immediately done. Years of experience have shown him how impossible it was, and how difficult it will be, to overcome the hostility of the predominant partner, and that it is not because a good case has been made out, and clothed with the authority of a Royal Commission, that redress will follow. His admitted integrity and wisdom, his long and faithful services to the cause of reform of Irish Taxation, his recognised authority and disinterestedness, add a special pathos to the appeal he made at Cork, which shall be the most fitting conclusion of this History :—

To a really united Ireland nothing could be refused ; and as the Financial Reform League has this unity for one of its principal objects, it is surely deserving of your support. Now, my lords and gentlemen, I have trespassed long on your attention, and it would be unpardonable on my part to occupy more of your time ; but I would fail in the chief object for which I came amongst you if I did not endeavour to impress upon you, as strongly as my poor abilities permit, the great, the far-reaching, the lasting importance of this unity of action. Why should not we be, at the end of this century, " United Irishmen " in the truest, the broadest, and, at the same time, the most constitutional sense ? The liberties which we enjoy, the powers which we can exercise, the influence which we can bring to bear on the whole government of this United Kingdom if we are only united, are so vast, so overwhelming, that, if but rightly used, they are irresistible. I ask you, then, to-day to form a branch of this association. I ask you to support it continuously, resolutely, perseveringly. I ask you to do so in the words of an address issued to your countrymen one hundred years ago—noble words, no matter what became the subsequent career of those who penned them. I ask you to endeavour to obtain a unity of mind and a knowledge of each other. To know each other is to know ourselves, the weakness of one and the strength of many. Union is, therefore, power ; it is also wisdom ; but it can be brought about by only one rule of conduct—to attend to those things in which we agree ; to exclude from our thoughts those in which we differ, remembering that nothing can be good for one part of the nation which has not for its object the interest of the whole.

APPENDIX.

TWO PETITIONS TO PARLIAMENT.

A.D. 1864.

Petition read at a meeting of the Dublin Corporation by Mr. John B. Dillon, on 8th February, 1864, unanimously adopted by the Municipal Council on 15th March, and presented in state by the Lord Mayor, Peter Paul M'Swiney, at the Bar of the House of Commons on 26th April, 1864 :—

TO THE KNIGHTS, BURGESSES, AND CITIZENS IN PARLIAMENT ASSEMBLED.

The Petition of the Lord Mayor, Aldermen, and Burgesses of the City of Dublin

Sheweth :

That by two returns made to your honourable House, dated respectively the 20th February, 1862, and the 30th June, 1863, it appears that the net ordinary revenue of Ireland, on an average of three years ending on the 31st December, 1862, amounted to £6,472,688. That the people of Ireland pay, in addition to the above sum, at least one million sterling in custom duties paid in British ports on articles consumed in Ireland, and a further sum of £200,000 from Crown rents and the Post Office, both of these sources of revenue being expressly excluded from the returns above mentioned ; and your petitioners therefore submit that the annual revenue now raised from Ireland somewhat exceeds £7,600,000. That, by the returns above referred to, the average amount of public expenditure in Ireland during the same three years appears to have been £3,905,838. That, in the expenditure as above stated, the advances made out of the Consolidated Fund for public objects are not included, neither are the repayments on account of said advances included in the income as above stated ; but your petitioners find by the same returns that during the three

years referred to the repayments exceeded the sums advanced by
£333,150. That a comparison of the income of Ireland with the expenditure will show that, of the revenue raised in this country, the
amount expended at home is very little over one-half ; the home
expenditure being £3,905,838, and the balance expended in England or elsewhere amounting to about £3,700,000. That, on an
average of ten years ending 1851, the public revenue paid in
Ireland amounted to only £4,400,000 per annum, as against an
average of £6,472,688 for the last three years ; and that, owing to
the great increase in our taxation, the annual remittances from
Ireland to England have grown during the last fourteen years from
about £700,000 to about £2,700,000. That the rents remitted
from Ireland to absentee proprietors are estimated by your petitioners to amount to between £3,000,000 and £4,000,000 annually ;
and that, accordingly, between absentee rents and the portion of
her income expended abroad, Ireland seems to be depleted to an
amount between seven and eight millions sterling per annum.
That the annual value of all the real property in Ireland, including
the houses of its towns and cities, as well as lands, amounts, by
official valuation, only to £12,324,853 ; and when this amount is
compared with that which is annually sent out of the country, we
cannot reasonably hope for the accumulation of capital, or the consequent growth of remunerative industry, as long as this ex-
hausting drain is permitted to continue. That, when the Act of
Union between Great Britain and Ireland was passed, the public
debt of Ireland amounted only to £26,841,219, the debt of Great
Britain being at the same time £420,305,944 ; and that, in sixteen
years after the passing of the Act of Union, Ireland was declared
liable for the entire of the British debt, incurred as well before as
after the Union, on the alleged ground that she had failed to pay
the proportion of the imperial expenditure which had been assigned
to her, while it was on all hands admitted that the proportion so
assigned to her was much larger than an impartial comparison of
her ability with that of Great Britain would have warranted. And
your petitioners feel that they re-echo a sentiment all but universally shared by the Irish people in expressing their dissatisfaction with an arrangement which subjected Ireland to an enormous
debt, in the contracting of which the representatives of the Irish
nation took no part, and from the expenditure of which the Irish
people derived no benefit. It would not be difficult for your petitioners, by a reference to past dealings with this country, to show
that some compensation is due to her ; but they will content themselves with declaring that, in the history of her connection with

Great Britain, they are unable to find any title in the latter country to the tribute which is now levied from the too scanty resources of Ireland. Your petitioners pray that your honourable House may, either by remission of taxes, or by increased expenditure in this country, establish a closer approximation than now exists between the income and expenditure of Ireland. And your petitioners will ever pray.

A.D. 1897.

The Municipal Council of Dublin, at their monthly meeting on 1st March, 1897, unanimously resolved to present a petition to Parliament. It was presented in state by Lord Mayor R. F. M'Coy on the 29th March. It was drawn up by Mr. Arthur W. Samuels, Q.C., and Mr. J. J. Clancy, Barrister-at-Law, M.P., instructed by the Law Adviser to the Corporation.

TO THE HONOURABLE THE COMMONS OF THE UNITED KINGDOM OF GREAT BRITAIN AND IRELAND IN PARLIAMENT ASSEMBLED.

THE PETITION OF THE RIGHT HONOURABLE THE LORD MAYOR, ALDERMEN, AND BURGESSES OF DUBLIN

SHEWETH:

That under the Treaty of the Union between the kingdoms of Great Britain and Ireland a constitutional right is guaranteed to Ireland to have her circumstances specially considered in reference to the imposition of taxation by the Parliament of the United Kingdom and to the incidence of such taxation.

That this right has been constantly and continuously insisted upon in Parliament by the representatives of Ireland of all political parties since the Union.

That the final report of Her Majesty's Commissioners appointed by Royal Warrant of 26th May, 1894, to inquire into the Financial Relations of Great Britain and Ireland establishes, nevertheless, the fact that, whilst the actual tax revenue of Ireland is about one-eleventh of that of Great Britain, the relative taxable capacity of Ireland is very much smaller, and is not estimated by any of the Commissioners as exceeding one-twentieth; and, consequently, Ireland is now taxed to an amount of between two and a-half and three millions pounds per annum in excess of her proper proportion.

That this grave injustice to Ireland, as further appears from the said report, has been brought about not only by the imposition of a financial burden at the time of the Union which, as events

M

showed, she was unable to bear, but by a serious addition to that
burden in 1853 and several succeeding years, which was not
justified by the circumstances of Ireland, but which, nevertheless,
has been continued and even increased since that time.

That this burden of excessive taxation has seriously injured, and
is seriously injuring, the material interests of Ireland, and has contributed in no small degree to retard her commercial progress and
prevent her industrial development, and that so long as it exists it
must continue to have that result, and to constitute a grave national
grievance affecting all classes of the Irish population.

That your petitioners feel confident that, in laying these views
before your honourable House, they are giving expression to con-
victions firmly held and well nigh universally entertained by the
citizens of Dublin.

Your petitioners therefore pray that your honourable House will
take into consideration the grievance disclosed by the said report,
and will, at an early date, adopt such measures as justice may
dictate to redress that grievance and to alleviate its effects. And
your petitioners will ever pray.

LORD LIEUTENANTS OF IRELAND,

1853 TO 1897.

1853. GEORGE EARL OF CARLISLE.
1858. ARCHIBALD EARL OF EGLINTON.
1859. GEORGE EARL OF CARLISLE.
1864. JOHN LORD WODEHOUSE, afterwards EARL OF KIMBERLEY.
1866. JAMES MARQUIS OF ABERCORN, afterwards DUKE.
1868. JOHN EARL SPENCER.
1874. JAMES DUKE OF ABERCORN.
1876. JOHN DUKE OF MARLBOROUGH.
1880. FRANCIS EARL COWPER.
1882. JOHN EARL SPENCER.
1885. HENRY EARL CARNARVON.
1886. JOHN EARL OF ABERDEEN.
1886. CHARLES MARQUIS OF LONDONDERRY.
1889. LAWRENCE EARL OF ZETLAND.
1892. ROBERT BARON HOUGHTON, afterwards EARL CREWE.
1895. GEORGE EARL CADOGAN.

CHANCELLORS OF THE EXCHEQUER,

FROM 1852 TO 1897.

1852. W. E. GLADSTONE, 28th December.
1855. SIR GEORGE C. LEWIS, 5th March.
1858. BENJAMIN DISRAELI, 27th February.
1859. W. E. GLADSTONE, June.
1866. BENJAMIN DISRAELI, 6th July.
1868. GEORGE WARD HUNT, 29th February.
1868. ROBERT LOWE, 9th December.
1873. W. E. GLADSTONE, August.
1874. SIR STAFFORD NORTHCOTE, 21st February.
1880. W. E. GLADSTONE, 28th April.
1882. H. C. E. CHILDERS, December.
1885. SIR M. HICKS-BEACH, 24th June.
1886. SIR W. V. HARCOURT, 6th February.
1886. LORD RANDOLPH CHURCHILL, 26th July.
1887. GEORGE J. GOSCHEN, 3rd January.
1892. SIR W. V. HARCOURT, 18th August.
1895. SIR M. HICKS-BEACH, July.

SPEECHES OF IRISH MEMBERS ON THE BUDGET OF 1853.

MR. W. T. FAGAN.

EXTRACTS FROM A SPEECH MADE BY WILLIAM TRANT FAGAN, MEMBER FOR CORK CITY, ON 25TH APRIL, 1853, IN THE HOUSE OF COMMONS. Mr. Fagan was a merchant and Alderman of Cork, and had filled the office of Mayor of that city. He was a Repealer.

He freely admitted that the superstructure of the financial scheme of the right hon. gentleman was grand—statesmanlike ; but the keystone of the arch on which it was erected was the inquisitorial income tax to be extended to Ireland—not to Ireland prosperous and prospering, but to Ireland downtrodden and struggling from the sad effects of a five years' famine. He felt it, therefore, a duty to his constituents and to the country of which he was one of the representatives, to offer the proposition the most strenuous opposition.

*　　*　　*　　*　　*　　*　　*　　*

He had shown, then, that for the benefits conferred on Ireland by the continuance in times of peace of an income tax she already pays her quota, without the necessity of extending that tax to Ireland. But he proposed to go further and show that, by the solemn treaty of the Union, Ireland was not bound to contribute to the general expenditure beyond her relative ability with the ability of England, to be ascertained by certain fixed and unalterable *criteria*. That was the principle on which the financial portion of the Act of Union was based. Taking these *criteria* as the basis of the calculations, it was ascertained and settled at the Union that Ireland's contribution to the general expenditure should be two-seventeenths ; that, in case the relative ability of both countries should alter, there should be a revision of the proportion to be contributed in periods of twenty years, unless in the meantime the debts of the two countries, which at the Union were at the ratio of 1 to 16, should approximate to 1 to $7\frac{1}{2}$, in which case the two exchequers should be consolidated, and thenceforward there should be a common taxation.

* * * * * * * *

Thus one (debt) increased four times (Ireland's), while the other increased but one-half (England's). This proved beyond question that the principle of the Union—namely, that each country should contribute according to its ability—was violated from the very commencement of that Act. The consequence was that, before the period of revision came round, the two debts had approximated to the relative proportion of 1 to $7\frac{1}{2}$, and the Exchequers were consolidated in 1816. This never could have occurred had Ireland only contributed according to the solemn contract she had entered into. Her relative ability to contribute would be periodically revised, and they would now be in a position, under the force of the Union Act, to ascertain and determine the fair proportion she should be called upon to pay.

* * * * * * * *

Why, since 1815, while £51,000,000 of taxes have been taken off the shoulders of England, Ireland has received a relaxation amounting to only £2,900,000 sterling up to 1846. He had now established beyond question that, both before and after the consolidation of the Exchequers, Ireland ought not to be forced to pay more than her relative ability to the general taxation, that ability to be ascertained according to the *criteria* set forth in the seventh article of the Union—namely, her relative income and her relative consumption of beer, spirits, sugar, wine, tea, and tobacco. Now, the ratio of Ireland's consumption to that of England's in these articles is as follows:—Beer, 1 to 25 ; spirits, 1 to 3 ; sugar, 1 to 15 ; wine, 1 to 12 ; tea, 1 to 9 ; tobacco, 1 to 6. This gives an average consumption of 1 to $11\frac{1}{2}$. Well, the income of England is ascertained to be £250,000,000. The income of Ireland is about £20,000,000, or $12\frac{1}{2}$ to 1. The compound ratio, then, of consumption and of income is 12 to 1, being England's ability relatively to Ireland to contribute to the general expenditure, which amounts to £52,000,000. Ireland pays into the Exchequer, exclusive of unacknowledged taxes, £4,000,000 a year, being one-twelfth of £48,000,000, England's contribution. Her unacknowledged taxation—that is, the duties paid in England on tea, sugar, wine, tobacco, coffee consumed in Ireland—is computed

to be nearly £1,000,000 a year.   Consequently, Ireland pays now
more than she ought under the terms of her treaty with England,
independently of her local taxation, which, including county cess,
poor rates, and municipal taxes, amounts to £2,000,000 a year, or
five shillings in the pound on the saleable property in Ireland,
while England's local taxation is but £12,000,000 on £100,000,000
saleable property, being less than 2s. 4d. in the pound.

MR. ISAAC BUTT.

EXTRACT FROM THE SPEECH DELIVERED BY MR. ISAAC BUTT IN
THE HOUSE OF COMMONS ON 2ND MAY, 1853.   Mr. Butt was
then a Conservative member.

If they were to have the income tax as an imperial tax, then he
would ask the committee to go fairly into the whole question of
the financial relations of Ireland.   He would ask them to consider
what was its local taxation, and what share of the national debt
Ireland in justice would be said to owe.   Let them appoint a committee to inquire into that subject, and he ventured to say that no
man would come out of that committee without the impression that
Ireland was over-taxed.

MR. THOMAS CONOLLY.

EXTRACT FROM A SPEECH OF MR. THOMAS CONOLLY IN THE
HOUSE OF COMMONS ON 2ND MAY, 1853.   Mr. Conolly was
a Tenant Right member.

Statistics would show that that country (Ireland) already paid
her full share of taxation, and that the claim for any greater
amount was devoid of justice.   The gross income of Ireland was
calculated at £20,000,000, whereas the gross income of Great
Britain, according to the authority of the right hon. baronet the
member for Halifax (Sir C. Wood), then Chancellor of the Exchequer, was stated at £250,000,000.   He took that to be the
proportion which the taxation of Ireland ought to bear to that of
Great Britain, or about 1 to 12½.   The gross revenue of the empire
was £52,000,000, of which Great Britain contributed £47,840,000,
and Ireland £4,160,000.   Now, the net produce of the Irish
revenue, on an average of ten years from 1835 to 1844, was
£1,164,000, so that Ireland had been paying a small amount above

her quota in proportion to her gross annual income. And yet it
was now proposed to violate the Union compact by materially
adding to the burdens of Ireland, and thus destroying that relative
proportion which ought to exist.

LORD CLAUD HAMILTON.

EXTRACT FROM A SPEECH OF LORD CLAUD HAMILTON, DELIVERED
IN THE HOUSE OF COMMONS ON 23RD MAY, 1853. Lord
Claud Hamilton was a Conservative member.

The right hon. gentleman (Mr. Gladstone) had relied on the old
story of the remission of the consolidated annuities. But the right
hon. gentleman knew well he never could have got the whole of
the annuities after the report and evidence on that subject printed
by the other House of Parliament. Giving him credit, however,
for the whole, the remission was not half the amount of the income
tax. Would the right hon. gentleman, with all his skill in ciphers,
show that this was a benefit to Ireland? Then, as to the spirit
duty, how could the Irish people be materially benefited? Had
not the experience of 1842 shown what would be the result of
that measure? Had the right hon. gentleman attempted to answer
all those arguments, it would not have been necessary to re-advert
to them. The right hon. gentleman was bound to defend his
financial position, but had failed to do so. The position of Ireland
was exceptional, and the taxation to be imposed would most probably be permanent. If there was to be a permanent tax riveted
on the country under pretence of a temporary tax, the condition
of the country ought to be investigated, and some endeavour
made to vindicate the policy proposed. It was only the right hon.
gentleman's evasion of all these topics which had created the
necessity for noticing them again at a late period of the evening,
when the House was far more full than when they had first been
brought forward. There was a derangement of the balance of
taxation between the two countries, which had been arranged at
the time of the Union as the basis of their financial positions.
The terms then agreed upon were that the two countries were
to unite as to future expenses on a strict measure of relative
ability. He would not go into the figures. The right hon. gentleman proposed a new scheme affecting the fiscal relations between
the two countries. The total amount of remission to England,
after deducting the £250,000 of additional income tax, was

£1,200,000, and the amount of increase of taxation applicable exclusively to Ireland was £658,000, which, after deducting the £200,000 remission of consolidated annuities, left an increase of taxation to Ireland of £458,000, thus granting large remissions to England, while imposing new and heavy burdens on Ireland. How could the right hon. gentleman justify this disproportion?

EARL OF MAYO.

EXTRACT FROM A SPEECH DELIVERED BY LORD NAAS, AFTERWARDS EARL OF MAYO, IN THE HOUSE OF COMMONS, ON 27TH MAY, 1853.

He believed that the tax-paying capability of Ireland was much greater then (1845) than it was at present, and therefore the objections of those high financial authorities would prevail and apply with far greater force now ; and to show this, it was only necessary to remind the committee that the circulation of Ireland was one-third less than it was in 1845; that the exportation of cattle and corn was almost nearly one-third less; and that, whereas in 1845 3,000,000 quarters of grain and malt had been exported, only 1,324,000 quarters had been exported last year. So that, in point of fact, it was impossible to make out the case that the tax-paying capacity of Ireland had been enlarged since 1845. He was justified, therefore, in asking what were the causes which had enabled the Government to come to a different conclusion from that of the Government of 1845, and also what was the amount expected to be realized from an Irish income tax.

IRISH TAXATION MENTIONED IN PARLIAMENT.

—

1853, 25th May. By GENERAL DUNNE.
1860, 30th March. By GENERAL DUNNE.
1863, 12th June. By GENERAL DUNNE.

General Dunne's Select Committee sat during 1864-65, and reported in 1865.

1864, 26th February. By GENERAL DUNNE.
1865, 24th February. By MR. W. E. GLADSTONE.
1867, 9th July. By SIR JOSEPH N. M'KENNA.
1868, 13th March. By SIR JOSEPH N. M'KENNA.
1868, 16th July. By MR. O'BEIRNE.

General Dunne and Sir Joseph N. M'Kenna lost their seats at the General Election of 1868. Sir Joseph N. M'Kenna was re-elected in 1874.

1874, 1st May. By SIR JOSEPH N. M'KENNA.
1874, 2nd July. By MR. MITCHELL HENRY.
1875, 12th March. By SIR JOSEPH N. M'KENNA.
1876, 23rd May. By MR. MITCHELL HENRY.
1877, 5th June. By MR. MITCHELL HENRY.
1882, 18th April. By SIR JOSEPH N. M'KENNA.
1886, 23rd February. By SIR JOSEPH N. M'KENNA.
1886, 8th April. By MR. GLADSTONE and MR. PARNELL.
1890, 30th May. By MR. THOMAS SEXTON.
1890, 14th July. By MR. THOMAS SEXTON.
1890, 1st August. By MR. THOMAS SEXTON.
1890, 12th August. By MR. THOMAS SEXTON.
1890, 13th August. By MR. THOMAS SEXTON.

Mr. Goschen's Select Committee held one sitting, but was never re-appointed.

1891, 27th February. By SIR T. G. ESMONDE, BART.
1891, 27th April. By SIR T. G. ESMONDE, BART.
1891, 11th June. By MR. THOMAS SEXTON.
1891, 18th June. By MR. H. H. FOWLER.

1891, 22nd June. By Mr. Goschen.
1891, 23rd June. By Mr. Goschen.
1891, 9th July. By Mr. Thomas Sexton.
1892, 23rd February. By Sir Joseph N. M'Kenna.
1892, 3rd March. By Mr. Hunter.
1892, 8th March. By Mr. S. Evans.
1892, 21st March. By Dr. Clark.
1892, 22nd March. By Mr. A. O'Connor.
1892, 31st March. By Dr. Clark.
1892, 11th April. By Mr. H. H. Fowler.
1892, 5th May. By Mr. G. J. Goschen.
1892, 6th May. By Dr. Clark.
1892, 12th May. By Mr. G. J. Goschen.
1893, 10th February. By Mr. J. J. Clancy.
1893, 24th February. By Sir John Hibbert.
1893, 9th March. By Mr. Cochrane.
1893, 17th March. By Colonel H. Vincent.
1893, 9th May. By Lord R. Churchill.
1893, 15th May. By Mr. William Kenny.
1893, 16th May. By Mr. Cochrane.
1893, 22nd June. By Mr. Gladstone.
1893, 3rd July. By Mr. Provend.
1893, 11th July. By Mr. Goschen.
1893, 13th July. By Mr. J. E. Redmond.
1893, 21st July. ⎫
1893, 24th July. ⎪ Financial Clauses
1893, 25th July. ⎬ of
1893, 26th July. ⎪ Home Rule
1893, 27th July. ⎭ Bill.
1893, 25th August. By Mr. Cochrane.
1893, 1st September. By Mr. J. E. Redmond.
1893, 1st December. By Mr. T. Sexton.
1894, 12th January. By Mr. Sexton.
1894, 13th February. Colonel Nolan.
1894, 13th March. By Mr. J. E. Redmond.
1894, 19th March. By Mr. J. J. Clancy.
1894, 19th April. By Mr. W. Field.
1894, 30th April. By Mr. L. Hayden.
1894, 4th May. By Mr. L. Hayden.

The Royal Commission sat during 1894-95-96, *and reported in* 1896.

1897, 21st January. By Mr. M. Ferguson.
1897, 22nd January. By Dr. Clark.
1897, 26th January. By Sir W. Dunne.
1897, 29th January. By Sir T. G. Esmonde, Bart.

APPENDIX.

1897, 2nd February. By Mr. J. Dillon.
1897, 8th February. By Mr. D. MacAleese.
1897, 9th February. By Mr. J. J. Clancy.
1897, 11th February. By Mr. J. Dillon.
1897, 12th February. By Mr. P. O'Brien.
1897, 16th February. By Mr. Vesey Knox.
1897, 18th February. By Mr. J. H. Dalziel.
1897, 22nd February. By Mr. J. E. Redmond.
1897, 23rd February. By Mr. J. J. Clancy.
1897, 5th March. By Lord Castletown.
1897, 18th March. By Mr. J. Dillon.
1897, 29th March. By Mr. Blake.
1897, 22nd July. By The Earl of Mayo.

INDEX.

N

C. W. Gibbs & Son, Printers, Dublin.

www.ingramcontent.com/pod-product-compliance
Lightning Source LLC
Chambersburg PA
CBHW030839270326
41928CB00007B/1129